Sunset Ideas & Recipes for

Breakfast & Brunch

By the Editors of Sunset Books
and Sunset Magazine

Lane Publishing Co.
Menlo Park, California

The great beginnings —breakfasts & brunches

Breakfast can be fun and full of surprises. In fact, what meal benefits more from innovation than breakfast? On some mornings, cereals or bacon and eggs will do. But on other mornings, it's wonderful to have something exciting or new on the menu.

This book offers delectable surprises, as well as the favorite breakfast standards. Also included are recipes for soups, sandwiches, casseroles, meat, fish, and poultry. So often ignored as breakfast possibilities, they make nutritious and easy morning fare. And with these recipes at your fingertips, it's hardly an extra step to prepare brunch—which is, after all, just a midday combination of breakfast and lunch.

So whether you're planning a weekday breakfast-on-the-run, a grand weekend brunch, or something in between, this book provides it all—tempting and delicious recipes, flavorful and nutritious menus, and ideas for happy, relaxed entertaining. And because the emphasis is directed toward advance preparation, you'll be able to enjoy the occasion as much as family and guests will.

For their cooperation in sharing props and locations for use in photographs, we extend special thanks to the owners and staff at B. F. J.'s Collectanea; Cotton Works; House of Today; Mediterranean Market; Wm. Price McNutt, ASID; Peets Coffee, Tea & Spices Co., Inc.; Taylor & Ng; and Williams-Sonoma Kitchenware.

Supervising Editor: Elizabeth Hogan

Research and Text: Elaine R. Woodard

Special Consultant: Joan Griffiths
Assistant Editor,
Sunset Magazine

Photography: Nikolay Zurek

Photo Editor: Lynne B. Morrall

Design: Cynthia Hanson

Illustrations: Ellen Blonder

Front cover: Dutch Baby Pancake (page 44)
Photographed by Nikolay Zurek

Editor, Sunset Books: David E. Clark

Third printing February 1982

Contents

*TALL STACK of Basic Pancakes (page 49) is
generously topped with whipped butter and
warm Maple-flavored Syrup (page 52).*

SPECIAL FEATURES

Fruits & Beverages for fresh starters & finales

As eye openers or grand finales, fruits and beverages add beauty, flavor, and variety to any menu. Our tasty fruit combinations and imaginative beverages are geared for family fun breakfasts or for relaxing brunch entertainment. The recipes can be adapted to a group of four or a gathering of twenty, and they include a wide range of fruits for all seasons, some fresh and others canned.

You can serve fruit as a first course, an accompaniment, or a dessert course, or you can make it the highlight of your menu. For a festive mood, try our champagne orange cocktail or the strawberry-filled melon bowls. And don't overlook the pineapple fruit refresher. Pineapple shells make perfect serving containers and inviting centerpieces.

This chapter also features whole-meal blender drinks for those quick-getaway mornings. In addition, you'll find fruity hot and cold punches to serve a crowd, as well as specialty coffees that will make you want to relax and sip right through the afternoon.

Glazed Apples or Pears

Apples or pears are sliced into rings, then pan-cooked in a cinnamon syrup until tender. Slice the fruit rings just before cooking so they won't darken when exposed to the air. These glazed rings go well with pancakes, waffles, or egg dishes, and pan-fried ham slices.

- 3 large tart apples or ripe pears
- 2 tablespoons butter or margarine
- 2 tablespoons firmly packed brown sugar
- ¾ teaspoon ground cinnamon

Core unpeeled apples or pears and slice into 1-inch-thick rings. In a wide frying pan over medium heat, melt butter. Stir in brown sugar and cinnamon. After sugar dissolves, add fruit. Cook, turning gently with a wide spatula, for 7 to 10 minutes or until fruit is just tender. Serve warm. Makes about 4 servings.

Hot Spiced Fruit

Made mostly with canned fruits, this hot-fruit crowd pleaser can be enjoyed the year round. You can use it as a pancake or waffle topping with a dollop of sour cream, present it as a side dish with egg entrées, or serve it in a bowl topped with cream.

- 1 can (1 lb.) *each* peach halves, pineapple chunks, and pitted light sweet cherries
- 1 can (1 lb.) *each* pear halves and apricot halves
- 2 tart apples
- 3 tablespoons lemon juice
- ½ teaspoon *each* ground nutmeg and ground cinnamon
- ¼ teaspoon ground cloves
- ⅓ cup firmly packed brown sugar
- ¼ cup butter or margarine, cut in chunks
- 3 bananas
- 2 cups seedless grapes (fresh or canned)
  Sour cream or whipped cream (optional)

Drain and combine syrup from peaches, pineapple, cherries, pears, and apricots. Reserve 1½ cups of the combined fruit syrup; save remaining syrup for other uses, if desired. Turn drained fruit into a 2½-quart baking dish. Core and dice apples, mix with lemon juice, then gently toss together with drained fruit.

Stir together reserved fruit syrup, nutmeg, cinnamon, cloves, and brown sugar; pour over fruit. Dot fruit with butter. Cover and bake in a 350° oven for 20 minutes. Peel bananas and cut into chunks. Lightly stir grapes and bananas into baked fruit, cover, and bake for 5 more minutes. Serve hot with sour cream, if desired. Makes 12 servings.

Honey Crunch Baked Apples

(Pictured on page 11)

Warm or cool, these chewy granola-filled baked apples are delicious topped with cream. Choose a good baking apple such as Rome beauty, pippin, or golden delicious.

   6 large apples
   ⅓ cup *each* granola (page 85 or purchased) and
        chopped dates
   ¼ cup chopped walnuts or almonds
   ½ teaspoon ground cinnamon
   ¼ teaspoon ground nutmeg
   2 teaspoons lemon juice
   ⅓ cup honey
   3 tablespoons butter or margarine, melted
   ¾ cup apple juice or water
        Half-and-half (light cream)

Peel apples, if desired, and core; stand upright in a 9-inch-square baking pan. To make filling, combine granola, dates, walnuts, cinnamon, nutmeg, lemon juice, and 3 tablespoons of the honey. Spoon equal amounts of filling into center of each apple (pack filling in lightly). Combine the remaining honey with butter and apple juice; pour over apples.

Cover and bake in a 350° oven for 30 minutes. Remove cover and bake, basting with pan juices several times, until apples are tender when pierced (about 35 minutes longer). Serve warm or cooled. At the table, pass a pitcher of cream to pour atop each apple. Makes 6 servings.

Fresh Fig & Ricotta Tulips

This novel idea takes advantage of the shape as well as the flavor of figs to make an attractive and tasty accompaniment. The figs and lemon-flavored ricotta cheese filling can be prepared well ahead of serving time.

   12 medium-large ripe figs
    1 cup ricotta cheese
   ½ teaspoon grated lemon peel
   ⅛ teaspoon salt
   ¾ teaspoon vanilla
   ¼ cup sugar
    1 egg white
   12 unblanched whole almonds

Rinse figs and pat dry. Trim off stems. To open figs into tulip shapes cut each fig into 4 petals by cutting through fig from stem end to about ½ inch from other end. Cover and chill, if made ahead.

In a blender container, combine cheese, lemon peel, salt, vanilla, and 2 tablespoons of the sugar; whirl until smoothly blended.

In a bowl, beat egg white until very foamy; gradually add remaining 2 tablespoons sugar; beat until stiff peaks form. Gently fold beaten white into ricotta mixture; cover and chill up to 4 hours.

To serve, stand 2 to 3 figs upright on each plate. Gently open each fig, spoon about 2 tablespoons of cheese mixture into center and top with an almond. Makes 4 to 6 servings.

Figs Ambrosia

Fresh figs lend their mellow sweetness to this ambrosia variation.

   2 large oranges, peeled, white membrane removed,
        and sliced
   8 ripe figs, sliced
   ¼ to ⅓ cup sugar
   1 teaspoon lemon juice
   ¼ cup grated fresh coconut or flaked coconut

Place orange slices in a serving bowl, top with a layer of figs. Sprinkle sugar, lemon juice, and coconut over fruit; chill. Makes 4 servings.

Quick Avocado-Grapefruit Salad

Bottled Italian dressing is the short cut for this salad-in-a-hurry to serve on plates alongside an omelet or with pizza muffins (page 82).

   2 *each* medium-size grapefruit and avocados
        Butter lettuce leaves
        Bottled Italian-style oil and vinegar dressing

Remove peel and white membrane from grapefruit; lift out sections. Peel, pit, and slice avocado. Line 6 salad plates with butter lettuce leaves. Arrange slices of avocado and grapefruit sections on lettuce. Pass Italian dressing to pour over individual servings. Makes 6 servings.

Papaya & Pineapple Compote

Fresh and canned fruit are gently mixed together in this delectable, make-ahead compote. Serve plain or topped with sour cream or yogurt and crunchy granola.

(Continued on page 7)

1 *each* large papaya and pineapple
1 can (11 oz.) mandarin oranges, drained
2 cups seedless grapes
 Sour cream or yogurt (optional)
 Granola (page 85 or purchased), optional

Peel and remove seeds from papaya. Peel and core pineapple (see page 9). Cut each fruit into bite-size pieces. In a medium-size bowl, gently mix together papaya, pineapple, oranges, and grapes. Cover and chill, if made ahead.

At the table, pass bowls of sour cream and granola, if desired, to spoon atop individual servings. Makes about 12 half-cup servings.

Fruit-filled Honeydew

(Pictured on opposite page)

Cool green wedges of sweet honeydew, with sliced peaches and plump berries, are topped with a tart cream dressing.

 Cream dressing (directions follow)
1 ripe honeydew melon
4 peaches or nectarines
1½ tablespoons lemon juice
1 cup *each* blueberries and raspberries (or strawberries)

Prepare cream dressing. When ready to serve, cut melon into 6 or 8 wedges; discard seeds. Peel, pit, and slice peaches; coat with lemon juice. Top each melon wedge with peach slices and berries. At the table, pass cream dressing to spoon over fruit. Makes 6 to 8 servings.

Cream dressing. In a small bowl, stir together 1 cup **sour cream,** 1½ tablespoons **honey,** ½ teaspoon **dry mustard,** and 2 teaspoons **lemon juice;** cover and chill for at least 2 hours.

Minted Melon Balls

A combination of melon balls — cantaloupe, watermelon, honeydew, Crenshaw, or Persian — makes a colorful medley to show off in a clear glass salad bowl. Serve with a chilled, mint-flavored citrus syrup, and garnish with sprigs of fresh mint.

⅓ cup sugar
½ cup water
1½ tablespoons coarsely chopped fresh mint or 2 teaspoons dry mint
2 tablespoons orange juice
1 tablespoon lemon juice
8 cups assorted melon balls or bite-size pieces (see suggestions above)
 Mint sprigs (optional)

In a small pan over high heat, combine sugar and water; bring to a boil, stirring, until sugar is dissolved; then boil for 5 minutes. Remove from heat and pour over mint; cover and chill for about 1 hour. Strain syrup through a wire strainer and discard mint. Stir in orange juice and lemon juice; cover and chill.

To serve, pile melon balls in a serving bowl, arranging them in layers, if desired. Pour chilled syrup over melon balls and garnish with mint sprigs, if desired. Makes 6 to 8 servings.

Peaches with Raspberries

Regardless of the season, you can enjoy this delectable combination of flavors and textures. Use a small, rimmed bowl for each peach half to hold it securely.

½ cup whipping cream
1½ tablespoons powdered sugar
½ teaspoon almond extract
1 can (29 oz.) peach halves, drained
¼ cup sliced almonds
1 package (10 oz.) frozen presweetened raspberries, thawed

In a small bowl, whip cream with powdered sugar and almond extract; set aside. Place peach halves, hollow side up, in small, individual bowls. Fill each hollow with 1 teaspoon of the almonds, then evenly distribute raspberries and their liquid over almond-topped peach halves. Top each with 2 or 3 tablespoons of the flavored cream. Sprinkle tops with remaining almonds. Makes about 8 servings.

Strawberries with Sour Cream

Whole fresh strawberries dipped in a flavored sour cream sauce can make an elegant starter or a grand finale.

½ pint sour cream
½ cup sifted powdered sugar
2 tablespoons lemon juice
3 tablespoons orange-flavored liqueur
2 baskets strawberries

(Continued on next page)

FROM A SUMMER'S BOUNTY of fresh fruits comes a showy brunch entrée – fruit-filled Honey-dew with its creamy dressing (recipe above). Champagne Orange Cocktail (page 12), homemade Croissants (page 68), and rolled ham slices round out the menu.

In a small serving bowl, stir together sour cream, powdered sugar, lemon juice, and orange-flavored liqueur; cover and chill. Wash strawberries.

To serve, place bowl of sour cream sauce on a serving plate and surround bowl with berries. Or hull and slice berries and place in individual bowls, then pour about 2 tablespoons of the sauce over each serving. Makes about 8 servings.

Strawberry-filled Melon Bowls

Marinated strawberries fill cantaloupe hollows in this festive fruit starter. The night before, refrigerate the melons and prepare the orange syrup. The next morning, slice berries into syrup to marinate while you finish preparing the meal.

- 2 large oranges
- 1 cup water
- ½ cup sugar
- 2 tablespoons orange-flavored liqueur (optional)
- 1 basket strawberries
- 2 medium cantaloupes

With a vegetable peeler, remove zest (colored part of peel) from oranges. Cut zest into 1-inch-long, thin strips. In a pan, combine zest and water; simmer, covered, until tender (about 10 minutes); drain and set peel aside.

Ream juice from oranges (you should have about 1 cup). Place in pan and add sugar. Boil over medium-high heat, stirring frequently, until sauce is reduced to ¾ cup (about 15 minutes). Add orange peel and cook for 3 minutes longer. Cool; add liqueur, if desired; then cover and chill.

Up to 4 hours before serving, wash, hull, and slice strawberries; gently stir into syrup. Cover and chill.

Just before serving, cut cantaloupes in half, making a plain or a zigzag edge. Scoop out and discard seeds. Evenly spoon strawberries and syrup into the hollow of each melon half. Makes 4 servings.

Papaya Avocado Cocktail

This brunch eye-opener is a surprising combination of flavors and textures. Crumbled bacon provides a crunchy topping; lime juice adds tang.

- ½ cup unsweetened pineapple juice
- 2 tablespoons *each* salad oil and chili sauce
- 1½ tablespoons lime juice
- ⅛ teaspoon ground nutmeg
- 1 *each* large papaya and avocado
- 4 strips bacon, cooked, drained, and crumbled

Combine pineapple juice, oil, chili sauce, lime juice, and nutmeg; set aside. Cut papaya in half crosswise and remove seeds; with a melon ball cutter, scoop fruit into balls, or peel and dice. Cut avocado in half crosswise; pit, peel, and slice. Combine papaya and avocado in a medium-size bowl. Pour dressing over fruit, cover, and chill for at least 1 hour.

To serve, evenly spoon fruit and dressing into sherbet glasses; sprinkle with crumbled bacon. Makes 4 to 6 servings.

Pineapple Fruit Refresher

Pineapple shells make attractive serving containers for this combination of fresh fruit. Vary the fruit according to your preference and what's available. You can arrange these inviting fruit-filled containers in the center of the table while you eat the entrée; then pass them for the finale.

- 1 medium-size pineapple
- 2 *each* bananas and peaches or nectarines
  Lemon juice
- 1 cup *each* strawberries and honeydew or casaba melon cubes
- 2 tablespoons honey
- 1 tablespoon cream-style peanut butter
- 1 cup unflavored yogurt
  Toppings: chopped peanuts, granola, or toasted coconut

Cut pineapple in half lengthwise. Leaving a ½-inch-thick shell, cut out fruit from each half and cut fruit into cubes (see page 9). Peel bananas and cut into ½-inch-thick diagonal slices. Peel, pit, and slice peaches (no need to peel nectarines, if used). Sprinkle bananas and peaches with lemon juice. Gently toss together pineapple, bananas, peaches, strawberries, and melon cubes; pile into pineapple shells. Cover and chill for as long as 2 hours.

In a small bowl, stir together honey and peanut butter; blend into yogurt. Cover and chill, if made ahead.

At the table, serve fruit from pineapple shells; pass yogurt sauce and your choice of toppings in individual bowls. Makes 4 to 6 servings.

Gingered Tropical Fruit Plate

Individual plates of fresh fruit salad feature thick slices of banana, wedges of papaya, and rounds of pineapple and orange — all topped with a creamy ginger dressing. This colorful fruit salad can be a refreshing meal opener or dessert.

(Continued on page 10)

Four different ways to cut a pineapple

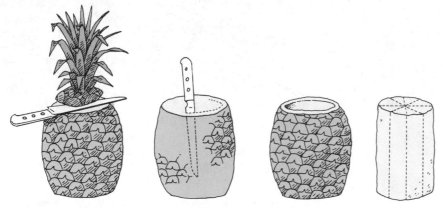

PINEAPPLE SPEARS OR ROUNDS. *With a sharp knife, cut away rind, a strip at a time. Remove pineapple "eyes" by cutting away diagonal strips. Cut fruit into spears or rounds to serve.*

PINEAPPLE RUBY. *Cut off top and save. With a sawing motion, cut completely around fruit, leaving a ½-inch shell at top. Remove cylinder; cut into spears. Return fruit to shell; place top back on to serve.*

PINEAPPLE BOATS. *Cut pineapple in fourths. Cut under core but not through ends. Slip a curved knife under fruit, loosening it from shell. Push out whole piece and cut crosswise into 6 or 8 pieces. Slip pieces under core in a zigzag pattern.*

PINEAPPLE SHELLS. *With a curved knife, cut around pineapple half, leaving a ½-inch-thick shell. Insert straight knife through core at a 45° angle. Cut out 4 wedges. Remove cores and discard. Cut fruit into chunks; pile back into shell.*

2 **bananas**
1½ **tablespoons lemon juice**
2 **oranges**
1 **medium-size pineapple, peeled, and cut in ½-inch rounds (page 9)**
1 **papaya, peeled, seeded, and cut lengthwise in ½-inch-thick slices**
  Red or green seedless grapes (optional)
  Lime wedges (optional)
  Ginger dressing (directions follow)

Peel bananas and cut into ½-inch diagonal slices; toss with lemon juice. Remove peel and white membrane from oranges and cut crosswise into thin rounds. On each of 4 plates, place 2 or 3 slices of banana, orange, pineapple, and papaya. Garnish with grapes and lime wedges, if you wish. Prepare ginger dressing and pass to spoon over individual servings. Makes 4 servings.

Ginger dressing. In a bowl, stir together 1 cup **sour cream** or unflavored yogurt and 1½ tablespoons *each* **honey** and chopped **candied ginger.** Cover and chill, if made ahead.

Buttermilk Fruit Ring

Studded with fresh fruit, this refreshing buttermilk fruit ring is an excellent choice for a buffet. Prepare it well in advance so there's ample time for it to gel. Garnish with whole fresh strawberries.

1 **envelope unflavored gelatin**
1 **cup *each* buttermilk and orange juice**
3 **tablespoons honey**
½ **small cantaloupe**
2 **peaches**
1 **cup sliced strawberries**
½ **cup chopped walnuts**
  Whole fresh strawberries for garnish (optional)

In a blender or food processor, sprinkle gelatin over buttermilk; let stand for 5 minutes to soften. Heat orange juice to boiling, then add to blender with honey. Cover container and whirl on low speed until well blended. Pour mixture into a bowl, cover, and chill until thick and syrupy (about 1 hour).

Cut rind off melon, discard seeds, and cut fruit into small pieces; you should have about 1½ cups. Peel, pit, and slice peaches. Stir cantaloupe, peaches, strawberries, and walnuts into gelatin mixture; pour into a 1-quart ring mold. Cover and chill until firm (at least 4 hours or overnight).

To unmold, dip in warm (not hot) water for about 10 seconds; run a knife tip around edge to loosen. Place a serving plate over mold; invert both and shake gently to loosen. Garnish with whole strawberries, if desired. Makes 4 to 6 servings.

Ginger Ale & Pear Mold

Pears and sparkling ginger ale are combined with lime gelatin in this simple and refreshing make-ahead mold. Use canned pears if fresh pears are unavailable. Serve alongside egg dishes.

1 **package (3 oz.) lime-flavored gelatin**
½ **cup boiling water**
1½ **cups ginger ale**
4 **large fresh pears or 8 canned pear halves, drained**
  About 1½ tablespoons lemon juice
  Sour cream or unflavored yogurt (optional)
  Mint sprigs (optional)

Dissolve gelatin in boiling water; stir in ginger ale. Chill until thick and syrupy.

Meanwhile, peel, halve, and core pears. Immediately brush surface of pears with lemon juice. Arrange pears, round side down, in a 1½-quart mold. Pour thickened gelatin over pear halves. Cover and chill until firm (about 3 hours).

To unmold on serving platter, follow directions in preceding recipe. Garnish with a dollop of sour cream and mint sprigs, if desired. Makes 8 servings.

Apricot Citrus

This quick and tangy beverage starts with canned apricot nectar; citrus juices make it come alive. Serve cold as a first course for breakfast or brunch. Garnish each glass with a sprig of mint, if desired.

2 **cans (12 oz. *each*) apricot nectar, chilled**
1 **tablespoon lemon juice**
3 **tablespoons lime juice**
½ **cup orange juice**
¼ **to ½ cup sugar**
  Mint sprigs (optional)

In a 2-quart pitcher, mix apricot nectar, lemon juice, lime juice, and orange juice; blend well, then add sugar to taste. Chill thoroughly. Pour into 4 or 5 glasses and garnish each with a mint sprig, if desired. Makes 4 or 5 servings.

BREAKFAST TO DELIGHT A CHILD includes Honey Crunch Baked Apples (page 5) and slices of Graham Yogurt Bread (page 61), served with wedges of cheese and a glass of cold milk.

Spiced Orange Tea Cooler

Zesty, candied ginger stimulates your taste buds in this cool, spiced, orange-flavored tea.

     2   large oranges
    ¼   cup orange-and-spice-flavored tea leaves
     1   quart boiling water
    ¼   cup chopped candied ginger
    1½ cups orange juice
     6   to 7 tablespoons sugar
         Ice cubes
     6   orange slices (optional)
         Mint sprigs (optional)

With a vegetable peeler, remove zest (colored part of peel) from oranges. Bruise zest with back of a spoon to release fragrance. In a tea pot, combine zest, flavored tea leaves, and boiling water. Cover and steep for 5 to 7 minutes. Strain; discard tea leaves and zest. Add chopped ginger to tea and let cool. Add orange juice and sugar; stir until sugar dissolves. Pour tea over 6 ice-filled glasses; garnish each glass with an orange slice and mint, if desired. Makes 6 servings.

Champagne Orange Cocktail

(Pictured on page 6)

Add a sparkle to your brunch with this elegant orange-flavored champagne.

     1   bottle (750 ml.) champagne, chilled
     4   cups orange juice, chilled
         Ice cubes (optional)

Just before serving, combine champagne and orange juice in a chilled pitcher or punch bowl. Add ice cubes, if desired. Makes about 14 half-cup servings.

Blender Yogurt Smoothies

Yogurt, fruit, and ice are whirled in a blender to make frosty, thick, and nutritious fruit shakes. You can use either whole-milk yogurt or low-fat yogurt. Sugar balances the tartness of the yogurt, so we give you a range. Start with the smaller amount of sugar and adjust the amount to suit your taste.

Strawberry-banana smoothie. In a blender, whirl until smooth: 1 cup *each* cracked **ice** and unflavored **yogurt;** 2 cups sliced **strawberries;** 1 **banana,** peeled and sliced; and 3 to 4 tablespoons **sugar.** Makes 2 or 3 servings.

Peach smoothie. In a blender, whirl until smooth: 1 cup *each* cracked **ice** and unflavored **yogurt,** 2 cups sliced **peaches** (fresh or frozen and partially thawed), 2 drops **almond extract,** and 2 to 3 tablespoons **sugar.** Makes 2 or 3 servings.

Tropical smoothie. In a blender, whirl until smooth: 1 cup *each* cracked **ice** and unflavored **yogurt;** 1 can (8 oz.) unsweetened crushed **pineapple,** drained; 1 **banana,** peeled and sliced; and 1 to 2 tablespoons **sugar.** Makes 2 or 3 servings.

Papaya smoothie. In a blender, whirl until smooth: 1 large **papaya,** peeled, halved, seeded, and cut into small chunks; 1 cup *each* cracked **ice** and unflavored **yogurt;** 1 to 2 tablespoons **sugar;** and 1 small **orange,** peeled, sectioned, and coarsely chopped. Sprinkle each serving with ground **nutmeg.** Makes 2 or 3 servings.

Meal in a Glass

(Pictured on page 62)

The alarm didn't go off, the children can't find their shoes, the suit you planned to wear needs pressing —the daily race to get out the door in the morning is sometimes delayed by these instant emergencies.

Blender breakfasts can make early morning pressures more tolerable. These meals you can drink afoot take only minutes to make and they're both satisfying and nourishing. Each has an egg or two as the base. Some are hot and light; others are cool, thick, and richly flavored with fruit. The ingredients can easily be cut in half or doubled.

Hot breakfast broth. In a small pan over medium heat, bring 2 cups **chicken broth** or beef broth just to simmering. In a blender, whirl 2 to 4 **eggs** until frothy. With the blender running, gradually add hot broth to eggs. Pour into 2 large mugs; top with grated **Parmesan cheese,** if desired. Makes 2 servings.

Coffees: For a grand finale

(Pictured on page 14)

The grand finale to any brunch is this elegant espresso coffee bar. Its success depends upon the staging. With a suggested menu of coffee specialties for guidance, guests can blend their own coffee house type of coffee.

It's not important to purchase an espresso machine or grind your own Italian or French roast coffee beans for a successful espresso ending. In most grocery markets you can purchase special espresso grinds in 1 and 2-pound cans. These special grinds can be brewed in American drip-pot coffee makers. Figure on using about 10 tablespoons of espresso grounds to about 2½ cups water.

If you don't know how strong your guests like their coffee, purchase a jar of instant espresso coffee which requires only a pot of boiling water. Allow at least two servings of coffee for each guest, but be prepared for greater demand. Supply one cup (demitasse or regular size) or mug for each guest.

Toppings. For each cup of coffee, allow about 1 tablespoon grated semisweet chocolate curls and about 2 tablespoons sweetened whipped cream.

Spices and seasonings. Provide a bowl or shaker of granulated or raw sugar; individual bowls of orange zest (colored part of peel removed from an orange with a vegetable peeler), whole cardamom pods, cinnamon sticks, whole nutmegs (with a grater); and shakers of ground cinnamon, ground nutmeg, and powdered chocolate.

Liqueurs and spirits. Present a bottle or decanter of brandy or Cognac, Kahlua (coffee-flavored liqueur), and crème de cacao. Allow about 1 ounce of liqueur for each cup of coffee.

Write out a menu of coffee specialties like the one that follows. Such a menu will provide suggestions for guests, but they can devise some combinations of their own, if they wish.

Mexican coffee: Coffee, cinnamon stick, whipped cream, and powdered chocolate or chocolate curls.

Parisian coffee: Coffee, cognac, and cream.

Brazilian coffee: Coffee, crème de cacao, cinnamon stick, whipped cream, and chocolate curls.

Caffé Borgia: Coffee, crème de cacao, whipped cream, and ground orange peel.

Cappuccino: Coffee, cream, ground nutmeg and cinnamon, and sugar.

Hot milk broth. In a small pan over medium heat, scald (stirring often) 2 cups **milk,** 1 teaspoon **butter** or margarine (optional), and 2 teaspoons **chicken or beef stock base** (or 2 chicken or beef bouillion cubes, crumbled). In a blender, whirl 2 to 4 **eggs** until frothy. With blender running, gradually add hot liquid to eggs. Pour into 2 large glasses or mugs; top with a dash of **pepper** (optional) and grated **Parmesan cheese.** Makes 2 servings.

Banana & fruit nectar. In a blender, whirl until smooth: 1 ripe **banana** cut into chunks, 2 **eggs,** and 1 can (12 oz.) **guava or apricot nectar.** (If fruit and nectar are warm, add crushed ice.) Pour into 2 tall glasses and sprinkle with ground **nutmeg.** Makes 2 servings.

Golden fruit whirl. In a blender, whirl until smooth: 1 cup drained canned **apricot halves** or sliced peaches (or partially thawed, frozen, sweetened peaches). Add 2 **eggs** and ¾ cup **orange juice**; whirl until smooth. Makes 2 servings.

Malted fruit nog. In a blender, whirl until smooth: 2 **eggs**; 1 cup *each* **milk** and **orange juice**; 2 tablespoons plain **malted milk powder**; 1 ripe **banana,** cut into chunks; and about ½ cup crushed **ice.** Makes 2 servings.

Orange & banana cream. In a blender, whirl until smooth: 2 ripe **bananas,** peeled and cut into chunks, 2 **eggs,** 1⅓ cup **orange juice,** and 1 cup **vanilla ice cream.** Makes 2 servings.

Orange froth. In a blender, whirl until smooth: 1 cup *each* **milk** and **water,** ¼ cup **sugar,** 1 teaspoon **vanilla,** 1 can (6 oz.) frozen **orange juice concentrate** (undiluted), 2 **eggs,** and 9 or 10 **ice cubes** (crushed). Makes 4 to 6 servings.

Strawberry nog. In a blender, whirl until smooth: 2½ cups sliced **strawberries,** 1 can (6 oz.) frozen **orange juice concentrate** (undiluted), 1½ cups **milk,** 1 cup crushed **ice cubes,** ¼ cup **sugar,** 1 teaspoon **vanilla,** 2 **eggs,** and 9 or 10 **ice cubes** (crushed). Makes 4 to 6 servings.

White Wine Sangría

White wine and citrus juices combine in this quick and cooling sangría. You mix it by the bowlful and keep it cold with a floating fruit-embellished ring of ice.

- ½ gallon cold dry white wine (such as Chablis or Chenin Blanc)
- 3 cans (6 oz. *each*) frozen lemon-limeade concentrate, thawed
- 1 can (6 oz.) frozen orange juice concentrate, thawed
- 2 cups cold water
  Ice ring (directions follow)

In a large punch bowl, stir together wine, lemon-limeade concentrate, orange juice concentrate, and water. Shortly before serving add ice ring. Makes about 25 half-cup servings.

Ice ring. Boil about 2 quarts of **water** (to clarify it) and let it cool. In the bottom of a ring mold no larger than your punch bowl, overlap slices of **lemon, orange,** or **lime,** or a combination. Pour about ¼ inch of the cooled water over the fruit and freeze until solid. Fill with remaining water and freeze. Unmold and float the ice, fruit side up, in the punch.

Creamy Apricot Nog

Apricot nectar makes a creamy punch that's not too sweet. This elegant punch begins with a cooked custard base that is then blended with cream, beaten egg whites, fruit nectar, and liqueur. If you want to make the punch without alcohol, note the alternative ingredients.

- 10 eggs, separated
- ¾ cup sugar
- ⅛ teaspoon salt
- ½ cup milk
- 1 cup whipping cream, whipped
- 1 large can (46 oz.) apricot or peach nectar
- 1 cup brandy or rum (or 1 cup more apricot or peach nectar and ½ teaspoon brandy or rum extract)
- ¼ cup orange-flavored liqueur (or 6 tablespoons thawed frozen orange juice concentrate)
  Freshly grated or ground nutmeg

In top of a double boiler, beat egg yolks until smooth. Stir in ½ cup of the sugar, salt, and milk. Cook,

GRAND BRUNCH FINALE stars an array of espresso coffee ingredients: Cognac, whipped cream, chocolate powder, cinnamon sticks, whole nutmegs, cardomom pods, orange peel, chocolate curls, sugar, and steaming hot coffee. Guests will probably invent their own variations, but you may want to provide a menu, as suggested on page 13.

uncovered, over simmering water, stirring occasionally, until custard thickens (about 15 minutes); let cool. In a large bowl, beat egg whites until frothy; gradually add the remaining ¼ cup sugar, beat until stiff peaks form. Pour cooled custard over whites and add whipped cream; gently fold together until blended. Add apricot nectar, brandy, and liqueur; mix gently to blend. Cover and chill for at least 3 hours or overnight.

To serve, beat mixture just until blended. Pour into a serving bowl and sprinkle with nutmeg. Makes about 20 half-cup servings.

Hot Chocolate

A hot cup of steaming chocolate is wonderful when there is a chill in the air. Top each cup with a dollop of sweetened whipped cream, if desired. To make Mexican chocolate, add a teaspoon of ground cinnamon to the milk mixture and top off each cup with a slender cinnamon stick.

- 6 cups milk
- 6 ounces unsweetened baking chocolate, shaved
- 6 tablespoons sugar
  Sweetened whipped cream

Combine milk, chocolate, and sugar; cook over hot water until chocolate melts and mixture is smooth. Beat with a wire whip or rotary beater until frothy. Pour into cups and top each with a spoonful of whipped cream. Makes 6 servings.

Hot Crimson Apple Punch

Pleasing both youngsters and adults, our nonalcoholic, hot spiced fruit punch is suitable for nippy winter days as well as chilly spring or summer mornings. This pretty crimson punch is an excellent buffet choice. Let guests start sipping the hot beverage while you put final touches on your menu. Serve along with creamy scrambled eggs (page 26) and a warm coffee cake.

- 1 gallon apple juice
- 2 quarts cranberry juice cocktail
- 3 whole cinnamon sticks
- 8 whole cloves
- ¼ cup lemon juice
  Thin orange slices

In a large kettle, combine apple juice, cranberry juice cocktail, cinnamon sticks, and cloves; bring to a simmer over medium-high heat. Pour into a large punch bowl and stir in lemon juice. Garnish with orange slices. Makes 1½ gallons.

Eggs Any Style

from poached eggs to omelets, soufflés to quiches

Is it a simple family breakfast you want, or an elegant weekend brunch? For either one, eggs are the ideal answer: they're always available, and almost always on hand in every refrigerator. With just a little know-how, almost anyone can transform them into nutritious, attractive, and delightful entrées.

This chapter offers you traditional egg entrées as well as innovative breakfast and brunch ideas. You'll find scrambled eggs simply garnished with parsley sprigs or lavishly embellished with a vegetable-clam sauce. You might choose eggs Benedict or a billowy soufflé. But whatever your choice, you'll find many tempting and satisfying recipes.

Use either white or brown eggs when you prepare these recipes; the nutritional value is the same. It is only the breed of hen that determines the color difference.

Avocados Huevos Rancheros

(Pictured on page 22)

For a dramatic brunch presentation, try these ranch-style eggs with a Mexican flavor. Chile-seasoned tomato sauce is spooned over softly poached eggs in avocado halves, then topped with melted cheese. The sauce and eggs can be made a day ahead. Serve avocados on a bed of shredded lettuce, with warm refried beans and corn or flour tortillas alongside.

- 2 tablespoons salad oil
- 1 medium-size onion, chopped
- 1 large can (about 15 oz.) tomato sauce
- 1 clove garlic, minced or pressed
- 3 tablespoons seeded and chopped canned green chiles
- 1 teaspoon *each* ground cumin and oregano leaves
- 1 bay leaf
  Salt and pepper
- 2 avocados
- 2 tablespoons lemon or lime juice
- 4 to 8 poached eggs (page 20)
- ½ cup shredded jack cheese
  Shredded lettuce

In a small frying pan over medium heat, add oil; when oil is hot, add onion and cook until limp. Stir in tomato sauce, garlic, chiles, cumin, oregano, and bay leaf. Reduce heat and simmer, uncovered, for 10 minutes or until slightly thickened. Season to taste with salt and pepper; remove bay leaf. If made ahead, cool, cover, and refrigerate until next day; reheat before serving.

Peel, pit, and halve avocados; coat cut sides with lemon juice and arrange, cut side up, in a 9-inch pie pan. Poach eggs or, if cooked ahead, reheat.

For each serving, lift 1 or 2 eggs from hot water, drain briefly, and arrange in the hollow part of an avocado half. Spoon 1 or 2 tablespoons sauce over eggs, and equally distribute cheese over sauce. Place in a preheated broiler about 6 inches from heat just until cheese melts. Serve each avocado half on a bed of shredded lettuce and pass remaining sauce to spoon over all. Makes 4 servings.

Poached Eggs with Chicken & Artichokes

Chicken and artichoke hearts in a rich and creamy sauce are the base for these poached egg ramekins. The sauce and poached eggs can be made a day ahead and rewarmed a few minutes before serving. Fresh fruit of the season and toasted English muffins make good accompaniments.

3 tablespoons butter or margarine
¼ cup finely chopped onion
3 tablespoons all-purpose flour
¼ teaspoon salt
⅛ teaspoon ground nutmeg
Dash of pepper
1½ cups half-and-half (light cream)
3 tablespoons dry sherry or chicken broth
3 cups diced cooked chicken
1 package (8 or 9 oz.) frozen artichoke hearts, cooked and drained
6 poached eggs (page 20)
1½ cups (6 oz.) shredded jack cheese
Chopped parsley

In a wide frying pan over medium heat, melt butter; add onion and cook until limp. Stir in flour, salt, nutmeg, and pepper; cook until bubbly. Gradually stir in half-and-half and sherry. Cook, stirring constantly, until thick and smooth. Gently mix in chicken and artichokes and heat through; or cool, cover, and refrigerate, if made ahead. Reheat to continue.

Poach eggs or, if cooked ahead, reheat. To serve, evenly spoon chicken mixture into 6 buttered ramekins. Lift eggs from hot water, drain briefly, and arrange an egg in each ramekin. Equally distribute cheese over each egg. Place in a preheated broiler about 6 inches from heat just until cheese melts. Sprinkle with parsley. Makes 6 servings.

Eggs with Asparagus & Chicken

(Pictured on page 19)

Eggs baked in a delicious blend of asparagus, chicken, and cheese sauce make elegant and hearty ramekins for four. Serve with warm croissants (page 68) or French bread and chilled melon wedges.

2 tablespoons butter or margarine
2 tablespoons all-purpose flour
¼ teaspoon salt
⅛ teaspoon *each* white pepper and ground nutmeg
1 teaspoon dry mustard
2 cups milk
1¼ cups (5 oz.) shredded Cheddar cheese
1 package (about 9 oz.) frozen asparagus pieces, cooked and drained
2 cups diced cooked chicken
4 eggs
4 teaspoons butter or margarine, melted and cooled
1 package (about 9 oz.) frozen asparagus spears, cooked and drained (optional)

In a pan over medium heat, melt the 2 tablespoons butter. Stir in flour, salt, pepper, nutmeg and mustard; cook until bubbly. Gradually stir in milk and

cook, stirring constantly, until thick and smooth. Stir in cheese until it is melted and the sauce is smooth. Stir in asparagus pieces and chicken; remove from heat.

Pour equal amounts of mixture into 4 buttered 1½ to 2-cup ramekins. Make a hollow in center of each and carefully break an egg into each hollow. Pour 1 teaspoon melted butter over each egg. Bake, uncovered, in a 375° oven for 15 to 20 minutes or until eggs are set to your liking. Garnish each ramekin with warm asparagus spears, if desired. Makes 4 servings.

Eggs Benedict

A traditional brunch entrée, eggs Benedict is as easy to prepare for 12 people as it is for two. It's simply a matter of making the components ahead, then putting them together to serve.

12 poached eggs (page 20)
¾ to 1 pound Canadian bacon or boneless cooked ham, sliced ⅛ to ¼ inch thick
6 English muffins, halved
Hollandaise sauce (directions follow)

Poach eggs or, if cooked the day before, reheat. In a wide frying pan over medium heat, cook bacon until lightly browned on both sides. Toast muffin halves and prepare hollandaise sauce.

To serve, place 1 or 2 muffin halves on each plate. Cover each half with bacon. Lift eggs from hot water, drain briefly, and arrange 1 egg over each bacon-topped muffin. Spoon about 2 tablespoons of hollandaise over each egg. Makes 6 to 12 servings.

Hollandaise sauce. Melt 1 cup (½ lb.) **butter** or margarine. In a blender or food processor, place 1 **egg** or 3 egg yolks, 1 teaspoon **Dijon mustard,** and 1 tablespoon **lemon juice** or wine vinegar; whirl at high speed until well blended. With blender running, add melted butter a few drops at a time at first, then increase flow to a slow, steady stream. Serve at once or, if made ahead, cover and refrigerate up to 1 week (bring to room temperature before reheating). To reheat, set container in hot, but not boiling, water; stir until smooth. Makes about 1½ cups.

Brunch Egg Nachos

Cheese melted over crisp tortilla chips makes a dish the Mexicans call *nachos.* Usually served as appetizers, they are transformed into delicious individual entrées when topped with sausage, eggs, and other garnishes. Most of the preparation can be done ahead for these easy-to-assemble-and-serve nachos.

½ pound bulk pork sausage
1 small onion, chopped
1 can (4 oz.) diced green chiles
4 cups crisp-fried tortilla pieces (directions follow) or corn-flavored chips
2 cups (8 oz.) shredded mild Cheddar or jack cheese
4 to 8 fried or poached eggs (page 20)
    Condiments. About ½ cup *each:* sour cream, guacamole or thawed avocado dip, sliced green onions, sliced ripe olives, prepared taco sauce

Crumble sausage into a cold frying pan. Place over medium-high heat, add onion, and cook, stirring, until meat is lightly browned; drain off fat. Stir in chiles, then set aside.

Divide tortilla pieces among 4 shallow 1½ to 2-cup ramekins or ovenproof bowls. Evenly distribute sausage mixture over tortilla pieces, then sprinkle ¼ cup of the cheese into each ramekin.

Fry or poach eggs. Place 1 or 2 eggs in each ramekin and sprinkle each with ¼ cup of the remaining cheese. Place in a preheated broiler about 6 inches from heat just until cheese melts.

At the table, pass sour cream, guacamole, onions, olives, and taco sauce to spoon over each serving. Makes 4 servings.

Crisp-fried tortilla pieces. Stack 6 **corn tortillas** and cut into 6 equal wedges. In a deep pan, pour **salad oil** to a depth of ½ inch and heat to 350° on a deep-frying thermometer. Fry 6 to 8 tortilla wedges at a time until crisp (1 to 1½ minutes). Remove with a slotted spoon and drain on paper towels. Cool, then package airtight if made ahead.

Sausage & Egg Cup

The egg and sausages in this simple-to-prepare recipe bake together in the oven in an individual custard cup or ramekin. We suggest ingredients for one entrée, but they can easily be multiplied for the number of people you intend to serve.

    Dry chervil or savory leaves
1 egg
1 teaspoon half-and-half (light cream)
    Salt and pepper
2 precooked tiny link sausages
    Paprika

Butter a 10-ounce custard cup or 1-cup ramekin. Sprinkle with chervil. Carefully break egg into the cup; top with half-and-half and sprinkle with salt and pepper. Arrange sausages around egg and

sprinkle with paprika. Bake in a 400° oven for about 10 minutes or until egg is set to your liking. (Baked eggs continue to cook slightly after removal from oven.) Makes 1 serving.

Baked Eggs in Tomato Shells

For a dramatic presentation at the table, try these simple eggs baked in tomato shells. You can prepare the rest of your menu while the eggs bake. Serve with sausage links and toasted English muffins or scones.

4 large firm tomatoes
1 teaspoon *each* salt, pepper, and dry basil
8 eggs
4 teaspoons grated Parmesan cheese
2 teaspoons chopped parsley
8 teaspoons butter or margarine, melted

Cut tomatoes in half crosswise. Leaving a ½-inch shell (be careful not to cut through the bottom), scoop out the pulp from each tomato half. (Save pulp and juice for other uses.) Invert tomato shells on paper towels to drain.

Place tomato shells, hollow side up, in a greased 9 by 13-inch pan; sprinkle each with salt, pepper, and basil.

Carefully break an egg into each tomato shell. Sprinkle each egg with ½ teaspoon of the cheese and ¼ teaspoon of the parsley, then drizzle 1 teaspoon butter over each.

Bake in a 350° oven for 20 to 25 minutes or until eggs are set to your liking. Makes 4 to 8 servings.

Baked Eggs & Mushrooms

Oven-poached eggs are baked in a mushroom sauce, then served on bacon-topped English muffins in this elegant brunch entrée. You can make the sauce ahead and reheat it before you add the eggs.

(Continued on page 23)

ROBUST MÉLANGE of cheese sauce, chicken, and asparagus is topped with a baked egg and more asparagus. The result: beautiful, nourishing Eggs with Asparagus & Chicken (page 17). Crusty French bread and chilled white wine are fine companions.

Egg cookery: The basics

A few simple rules of thumb are all you need to master the basics of egg cookery: Purchase only refrigerated eggs, and keep them refrigerated until you're ready to use them. Keep eggs covered in their original carton or another covered container; otherwise they pick up odors and flavors from other refrigerated foods. And use moderate temperatures —never high heat— in egg cookery.

Fluffy Scrambled Eggs

A little liquid added to eggs before cooking produces the tender, velvety-textured, golden mass known as scrambled eggs. Some people prefer their eggs dry and use no liquid at all, but we suggest adding 1 teaspoon to 1 tablespoon liquid for each egg, and ¼ teaspoon salt for every 2 or 3 eggs.

Break the eggs into a bowl, add liquid and salt, and beat with a fork until thoroughly blended but not frothy. Choose a wide frying pan to fit the amount of egg mixture to be cooked. Measure about ½ tablespoon butter, margarine, bacon fat, or salad oil per egg. Place it in a wide frying pan over medium-low heat. Keep the temperature constant —overheating makes scrambled eggs rubbery.

When pan is hot, pour in egg mixture. Cook eggs, gently lifting cooked portion to allow uncooked portion to flow underneath, until eggs are softly set. Use a wide spatula; this helps to maintain the wholeness of the golden mass and its light, smooth, creamy texture. Never rush eggs —they should cook slowly and gently. Remove pan from heat when eggs are still creamy; they will finish cooking in their own heat.

Fried Eggs

You can fry eggs in a nonstick pan as the manufacturer directs, but you'll most likely enjoy the flavor more if you use a little fat. Butter, margarine, bacon fat, or salad oil —the choice is yours.

It is important to fry eggs in a preheated pan over medium heat. This method gives you tender, evenly cooked eggs. If the heat or pan is too hot, the eggs cook on the bottom before they're set on the top, resulting in whites that are crisp, brown, and leathery.

Melt fat (1 to 2 teaspoons per egg) in a wide frying pan over medium heat. (Use two pans to cook more than 6 eggs at one time.) For well-shaped eggs, break each one directly into the pan, holding the shell almost against pan surface; lift shell away carefully to avoid stretching or tearing the egg. Over medium heat, eggs begin to set as soon as they touch the pan surface.

For over-easy style, just fry eggs on one side, then turn over and fry briefly on the other. Or for opaquely covered yolks, sprinkle 1 to 2 teaspoons water over each egg in pan (or baste eggs with the melted fat in pan), cover, and cook for about 2 minutes.

Soft or Hard-cooked Eggs

(Pictured on page 75)

Never boil eggs. If you do, you're courting such disasters as cracked and leaking shells, waterlogged and lopsided eggs, and rubbery whites.

A perfect soft-cooked egg has a tender white, solidified to the consistency you prefer, and a hot, liquid to semiliquid yolk. An excellent hard-cooked egg begins the same way, but the white is completely firm, yet tender; the yolk is firm and dry throughout, with the same color on the outside as in the center.

When cooking eggs in their shells, it's best to use eggs that are at room temperature to prevent the shells from cracking. If you do use eggs directly from the refrigerator, follow the directions below but increase the total cooking time by 2 minutes.

Place eggs, without crowding, in a single layer in a pan with straight sides. Fill just to cover with water. Set pan, uncovered, over high heat and bring water to simmering (bubbles will just begin to rise to surface of pan). This takes about 8 to 11 minutes.

For soft-cooked eggs, remove pan from heat when water begins to simmer; cover and let stand for 2 to 4 minutes. For hard-cooked eggs, reduce heat to medium when water begins to simmer; cook for 15 to 18 minutes. At end of specified time, drain eggs and immediately cover with cold water. This stops the cooking process.

To shell hard-cooked eggs, tap each egg gently all over on a flat surface or with the back of a spoon. Under running cold water, roll the egg between the palms of your hands to loosen the shell.

Poached Eggs

A good poached egg has a well-centered yolk snugly surrounded by the white and cooked just to the firmness you like. The best way to achieve this is to use a unique heat-set method that makes the egg more compact when it's poached. You heat-set the eggs by immersing them, still in the shell, in rapidly boiling water for exactly 8 seconds. The timing must be very accurate or the eggs will not slip easily out of their shells into the poaching liquid.

Fill a wide, greased frying pan with about 1½ inches of water. Add 1 teaspoon vinegar and heat until bubbles form on the pan bottom with an occasional one popping to the top. Break each heat-set egg into the water; do not overcrowd. Cook until set to your liking (poke white gently to check firmness). For soft yolks and firm whites, allow 3 to 5 minutes.

With a slotted spoon, lift eggs from hot water. To use eggs at once, drain briefly on paper towel.

To make poaching easier for entertaining, and to eliminate a lot of last-minute work, we suggest pre-poaching your eggs a day ahead and then reheating them at serving time.

To do this, immerse poached eggs in ice water as soon as you lift them from the hot water. Cover and chill for as long as 24 hours.

To reheat, transfer eggs to a bowl of very hot tap water for 5 to 10 minutes or until eggs are hot to the touch.

Light & Fluffy Soufflés

Soufflés have always had an aura of mystery about them, yet they are remarkably simple to make once you've mastered a few techniques. The ingredients for a main-dish soufflé are simply a thick white sauce, eggs, and your choice of vegetables, fish, poultry, meat, or cheese. Make your white sauce first and let it cool while you prepare your eggs.

Start with eggs at room temperature to achieve the greatest volume. Separate eggs carefully. If a bit of yolk falls into whites, remove before beating. If you cannot remove all traces of yolk, save eggs and use for another purpose. The slightest amount of fat from the yolk—or for that matter, an oily bowl or beaters—will decrease the volume of beaten whites.

Beaten whites should hold distinct but moist peaks. If whites are overbeaten and become dry, they will be difficult to fold into the sauce-yolk mixture.

To maintain the volume of the beaten whites, lighten the heavy white sauce by gently folding a portion of the beaten egg whites into the sauce. Then gently fold the sauce into remaining egg whites.

You do *not* need a traditional soufflé dish. Any straight-sided, deep, ovenproof baking dish will do, as long as the volume is the same as that stated in the recipe. The dish must be well greased.

Once your soufflé is assembled in the baking dish, put it directly into a preheated oven. Your oven *must* be preheated because the soufflé bakes from the bottom up and it needs quick bottom heat to achieve height.

The soufflé is done when the top is golden or feels firm to the touch, and jiggles only slightly when gently shaken. The French prefer their soufflés, like their eggs, moist and creamy. Americans, on the other hand, often prefer theirs more firm.

Once baked, your soufflé can remain in the turned-off oven for approximately 10 minutes before it begins to collapse. It will continue to cook slightly, however, and become more firm.

Omelets—Plain or Puffy

To make a plain omelet (also called a French omelet), do not separate the eggs; beat them whole, together with the liquid called for in the recipe. The puffy omelet is prepared by beating the whites and yolks separately and then folding them together. Both omelets are cooked on top of the range, but the puffy omelet finishes cooking in the oven.

Each omelet requires the same cooking technique. Heat pan over medium-high heat. Add fat and tilt pan to coat bottom and sides. Pour in egg mixture and cook, gently lifting cooked portion to allow uncooked portion to flow underneath. Shake pan frequently to keep egg moving freely. Omelet is done when egg is set but top still looks liquid and creamy. Remove from heat; omelet will continue to cook slightly in its own heat.

Plain omelets, especially with a filling, are often folded—either in thirds or in half. To fold an omelet in thirds, first spoon 2 or 3 tablespoons filling down center of omelet, in line with pan handle. Holding pan in your left hand, slide spatula under right edge of omelet, lift edge, and fold about ⅓ of omelet over filling. Switch pan to your right hand and, tilting right end up and holding pan over a warm serving plate, gently shake pan to slide unfolded edge of omelet just onto plate. Flick your right wrist downward so that previously folded edge of omelet (guided by your spatula) falls neatly over omelet edge on plate.

To fold an omelet in half, spoon filling over one half of omelet; run a spatula around edge of omelet, then tip pan and slide spatula under omelet to loosen it from pan. Fold omelet in half and slide out onto a warm serving plate.

4 tablespoons butter or margarine
½ pound mushrooms, sliced
⅓ cup chopped onion
¼ cup all-purpose flour
¾ cup chicken broth
¼ cup whipping cream
   Salt and pepper to taste
6 eggs
¼ cup grated Parmesan cheese
6 slices Canadian bacon
3 English muffins, halved
   Chopped parsley

In a frying pan over medium-heat, melt butter; set 2 tablespoons aside. Add mushrooms and onion to pan and cook until onion is limp. Stir in flour and cook until bubbly; gradually stir in broth and cream; cook, stirring constantly, until thick and smooth. Season to taste with salt and pepper.

Pour sauce into a shallow 2-quart baking dish. Break eggs onto sauce, carefully arranging in a circle; do not stir. Spoon reserved 2 tablespoons butter over tops of eggs, then sprinkle with cheese. Bake, uncovered, in a 350° oven for about 15 minutes or until eggs are set to your liking.

In a lightly greased frying pan over medium heat, cook bacon until lightly browned on both sides. Toast muffin halves.

To serve, arrange a slice of bacon on each muffin half. Spoon 1 egg and some sauce over each muffin and sprinkle with parsley. Makes 6 servings.

Chard-Sausage Scramble

In this quick and delicious interpretation of the classic Western favorite, Joe's Special, the traditional spinach and ground beef mixture is replaced with Swiss chard and Italian sausage. Serve it garnished with tomato wedges, and pass grated Parmesan cheese to sprinkle over the top.

1 package (about 10 oz.) frozen Swiss chard or chopped spinach, thawed
½ pound mild Italian sausages
1 large onion, chopped
1 clove garlic, minced or pressed
6 to 8 eggs
   Tomato wedges
   Grated Parmesan cheese

FOR BRUNCH WITH A MEXICAN FLAIR, consider colorful Avocado Huevos Rancheros (page 16), along with refried beans and warm rolled tortillas. Pass some of the sauce in a small bowl.

Squeeze as much liquid as possible from thawed chard; chop and set aside. Remove casings from sausages, crumble meat into a wide frying pan, and cook, uncovered, over medium-high heat until browned. Add onion and garlic; cook, stirring, until onion is limp. You may want to drain fat from pan at this point. Stir chard into pan; cook, stirring, until all liquid has evaporated (about 1 minute).

Beat eggs until blended; pour over chard mixture. Reduce heat to medium-low and cook, gently lifting cooked portion to allow uncooked portion to flow underneath, until eggs are softly set. Transfer eggs to a warm serving dish. Encircle with tomato wedges and serve with Parmesan cheese to sprinkle over individual servings. Makes 4 to 6 servings.

Scrambled Eggs with Clam Sauce

You can top gently scrambled eggs with a vegetable clam sauce to make a speedy family brunch. Serve with tomato slices and hot buttered rolls.

1 can (about 7 oz.) chopped clams
2 teaspoons cornstarch
4 strips bacon
½ cup *each* thinly sliced carrot and celery
2 tablespoons *each* chopped green pepper and thinly sliced green onion
8 eggs
1 tablespoon water
¼ teaspoon salt
⅛ teaspoon pepper
2 tablespoons butter or margarine

Drain clams and reserve ½ cup of the juice; set clams aside. In a small bowl, blend reserved clam juice and cornstarch; set aside.

In a frying pan over medium-high heat, cook bacon until crisp. Remove bacon from pan; drain, crumble, and set aside. Discard all but 2 tablespoons of the bacon drippings.

To the drippings, add carrot, celery, and green pepper; cover and cook over medium heat, stirring often, for 4 minutes or until carrot is just tender. Stir in clams and green onion. Stir clam juice-cornstarch mixture once, then stir into pan and continue stirring until thickened. Remove from heat and keep warm while you scramble the eggs.

Beat eggs with water, salt, and pepper. Melt butter in a wide frying pan over medium-low heat; add eggs and cook, gently lifting cooked portion to allow uncooked portion to flow underneath, until eggs are softly set. Transfer eggs to a warm serving dish, spoon clam-vegetable sauce over the top, and garnish with crumbled bacon. Makes 4 or 5 servings.

Brunch Egg Tostadas

Scrambled eggs, cheese, ripe olives, and avocado slices top a crisp-fried tortilla for this Mexican-style dish. Pass taco sauce to spoon over the warm tostadas.

 Salad oil
4 corn tortillas
6 eggs
1 canned green chile, seeded and chopped
4 tablespoons milk
 Salt and pepper
1 tablespoon butter or margarine
1 cup (4 oz.) shredded Cheddar or jack cheese
½ cup thinly sliced green onion
8 to 12 *each* avocado slices and ripe olives
 Prepared taco sauce

In a small frying pan over medium-high heat, add about ¼ inch salad oil. When oil is hot, fry 1 tortilla at a time until it crisps and browns lightly (15 to 30 seconds on a side); drain on paper towels and set aside.

In a bowl, beat eggs lightly with chile, milk, and salt and pepper to taste. In another frying pan, melt butter over medium-low heat. Add eggs and cook, gently lifting cooked portion to allow uncooked portion to flow underneath, until eggs are softly set. Arrange tortillas on a baking sheet, spoon eggs evenly over tortillas, then sprinkle with cheese. Place in a preheated broiler about 6 inches from heat just until cheese melts. Garnish each tortilla with onion, avocado slices, and olives. Serve with taco sauce to spoon over individual servings. Makes 4 servings.

Herb Eggs with Yogurt Sauce

For a Middle Eastern flavor, scramble eggs with herbs and top with a cool yogurt sauce that can easily be made a day in advance. Serve the eggs with sliced cucumbers, ripe olives, cherry tomatoes, and sweet rolls.

 Yogurt sauce (directions follow)
8 eggs
2 tablespoons water
¼ teaspoon pepper
½ teaspoon *each* salt and sugar
2 tablespoons butter or margarine
½ cup minced parsley
¼ cup minced green onion

Brunch extra: Potato casserole

When you think of eggs, is your next thought potatoes? If so, you'll enjoy this dish. A cross between hash-browned and scalloped potatoes, it is a good brunch accompaniment, and you can easily double the recipe for a buffet. It takes time to prepare, but you have almost an hour while it bakes to assemble the rest of your menu.

3 medium-size russet potatoes (about 1½ lbs.)
 Water
½ cup milk
3 tablespoons butter or margarine
2 eggs
1½ teaspoons salt
⅛ teaspoon pepper
1 large onion, chopped
 Paprika

Peel and shred potatoes; you should have 4 cups. Immediately transfer potatoes to a bowl. Cover with water to prevent discoloration; set aside.

Remove ¼ cup water from potatoes and place in a small pan with milk and 2 tablespoons of the butter; cook over medium heat to just under boiling; remove from heat and set aside.

Beat eggs with salt and pepper. Continue beating and slowly pour the hot milk mixture over eggs; blend well.

Drain potatoes well by pouring into a colander and pressing out the liquid. Combine potatoes, onion, and egg mixture. Rub the remaining 1 tablespoon butter over sides and bottom of a 9 by 13-inch baking pan. Spoon potato mixture into pan and sprinkle with paprika. Bake, uncovered, in a 375° oven until set in center and edges are browned and crusty (about 50 minutes). Cut in squares to serve. Makes 6 servings.

Prepare yogurt sauce; cover and refrigerate if made ahead. In a bowl, beat together eggs, water, pepper, salt, and sugar just until blended; set aside.

In a wide frying pan over medium-high heat, melt butter. Stir in parsley and green onion; cook, stirring, for 1 minute. Reduce heat to medium-low, pour in eggs, and cook, gently lifting cooked portion to allow uncooked portion to flow underneath, until eggs are softly set. Serve immediately with yogurt sauce to spoon over individual servings. Makes 4 servings.

Yogurt sauce. In a bowl, combine 1 cup **unflavored yogurt**, 2 tablespoons *each* minced **green onion** and **fresh mint** (or 1½ teaspoons dry mint), 2 teaspoons **lemon juice**, and a dash of **liquid hot pepper seasoning.**

Pizza-topped Eggs

Scrambled eggs are the base here for a pizzalike topping of herb tomato sauce and melted cheese. If your time is limited in the morning, prepare the tomato sauce a day ahead; simply reheat the sauce while you scramble the eggs. Serve with warm crusty rolls and chilled fresh fruit.

- 3 **tablespoons butter or margarine**
- ¼ **cup chopped onion**
- 1 **clove garlic, minced or pressed**
- 1 **can (about 15 oz.) pear-shaped tomatoes**
- ½ **teaspoon** *each* **dry basil and oregano leaves**
- 8 **eggs**
- 2 **tablespoons water**
- ¼ **teaspoon salt**
  Dash of pepper
- ¾ **cup shredded mozzarella cheese**

In a frying pan over medium heat, melt 1 tablespoon of the butter. Add onion and garlic; cook, stirring, until onion is limp. Add tomatoes and their liquid, breaking them up with a fork, and stir vegetables along with basil and oregano. Reduce heat and simmer, uncovered, stirring occasionally, for about 20 minutes or until sauce is thickened and most of the liquid has evaporated; set aside.

In a bowl, beat eggs, water, salt, and pepper. In a wide frying pan over medium-low heat, melt the remaining 2 tablespoons butter. Add egg mixture and cook, gently lifting cooked portion to allow uncooked portion to flow underneath, until eggs are softly set. Spoon eggs into a lightly buttered pan or ovenproof dish. Spoon tomato sauce over eggs and sprinkle with cheese. Place in a preheated broiler about 6 inches from heat just until cheese melts. Cut in wedges or squares; lift sections with spatula to serve. Makes 4 to 6 servings.

Make-ahead Layered Mushrooms & Eggs

This layered egg and mushroom dish is quick and easy to make ahead for a crowd. Serve it with crisp bacon strips or link sausages, a fruit punch, and warm coffee cake.

- 1 **can (about 10¾ oz.) condensed cream of mushroom soup (undiluted)**
- 3 **tablespoons dry sherry or milk**
- 1½ **cups (6 oz.)** *each* **shredded sharp Cheddar cheese and jack cheese**
- 18 **eggs**
- 2 **tablespoons milk**
- 1 **teaspoon parsley flakes**
- ½ **teaspoon dill weed**
- ⅛ **teaspoon pepper**
- 4 **tablespoons butter or margarine**
- ¼ **pound mushrooms, sliced**
- ¼ **cup chopped green onion**
  Paprika

In a pan over medium heat, stir soup and sherry until hot and smooth. Remove from heat and set aside. In a small bowl, toss cheeses lightly to mix; set aside. Beat together eggs, milk, parsley, dill weed, and pepper; set aside.

In a wide frying pan over medium-low heat, melt butter. Add mushrooms and onion and cook, stirring, until onion is limp. Add egg mixture and cook, gently lifting cooked portion to allow uncooked portion to flow underneath, until eggs are softly set; remove from heat. Spoon half the scrambled eggs into a 7 by 11-inch baking dish. Spoon half the soup mixture over the eggs, then sprinkle evenly with half the cheese mixture. Repeat layers; sprinkle top with paprika. If made ahead, cool, cover, and refrigerate until next day.

Bake, uncovered, in a 300° oven for 30 to 35 minutes (1 hour, if refrigerated) or until hot and bubbly. Let stand for about 10 minutes, then cut into squares. Makes 8 to 10 servings.

Mexican-style Scrambled Eggs

Spiced tamales hide under scrambled eggs covered with melted cheese in this quick-to-assemble dish. Serve it plain or with sour cream, green pepper, olives, and avocado.

    1 can (about 15 oz.) tamales
    8 eggs
    2 tablespoons milk
    ½ teaspoon salt
    2 tablespoons butter or margarine
    2 cups (8 oz.) shredded Cheddar cheese
       Condiments. About ½ cup each: sour cream,
         chopped green pepper, sliced ripe olives, and
         diced avocado

Drain tamales, reserving half the sauce from the can. Remove wrappings from tamales. Cut each tamale into 3 equal-size pieces; arrange on a heatproof serving plate. Pour reserved sauce over tamales. Place tamales in a 350° oven for about 10 minutes.

Meanwhile, prepare the eggs. Beat eggs lightly with milk and salt. In a wide frying pan over medium-low heat, melt butter. Pour in eggs and cook, gently lifting cooked portion to allow uncooked portion to flow underneath, until eggs are softly set.

Remove tamales from oven, spoon eggs over tamales, and sprinkle cheese over all. Place in a preheated broiler about 6 inches from heat just until cheese melts. Serve condiments in separate bowls to spoon over eggs. Makes 4 to 6 servings.

Creamy Scrambled Eggs

(Pictured on opposite page)

Here is an excellent entrée for a buffet. Most eggs must be served immediately after cooking, but you can keep these eggs creamy and warm for as long as an hour on an electric warming tray. Then let each person choose from an interesting variety of condiments to embellish the eggs. For a unique and unusual brunch entrée, serve these eggs in baked potato boats (page 79).

    4 tablespoons butter or margarine
    2 tablespoons all-purpose flour
    1 cup sour cream
    2 dozen eggs
    ¾ teaspoon salt
    ⅛ teaspoon white pepper
       Chopped parsley
       Condiments. About 1 cup each: crisp bacon
         bits, shredded Cheddar cheese or blue-veined
         cheese, sliced ripe olives, sliced green onions,
         small cooked shrimp, caviar, and sour cream

In a small pan over medium heat, melt 2 tablespoons of the butter. Stir in flour and cook until bubbly. Remove from heat and blend in sour cream. Return to heat and cook until bubbly and smooth; set aside.

Beat together eggs, salt, and pepper. In a wide frying pan over medium-low heat, melt the remaining 2 tablespoons butter; pour in eggs and cook, gently lifting cooked portion to allow uncooked portion to flow underneath, until eggs are softly set. Remove from heat and gently stir in sour cream mixture.

Turn eggs into a serving dish and garnish with parsley. Keep warm on an electric warming tray for as long as 1 hour. Serve condiments in individual bowls. Makes about 12 servings.

Scotch Baked Eggs

This egg-sausage combination is simple, quick, and delicious. You can wrap the hard-cooked eggs in sausage a day ahead, then just pop them into the oven for 30 minutes before serving. To take Scotch eggs on a picnic, wrap them individually in foil after baking; they'll keep warm for a half-hour.

    1¼ pounds bulk pork sausage
     4 hard-cooked eggs (page 20), chilled and shelled

Divide sausage into 4 equal portions and, on wax paper, flatten each portion into a round flat cake about ⅜ inch thick. Loosen patties from paper with a spatula. Moisten your hands for easier handling of sausage and wrap each egg completely in the sausage; smooth surfaces until free from cracks. (If made ahead, cover and refrigerate until next day.)

Place sausage-wrapped eggs slightly apart in a shallow pan. Bake in the upper third of a 450° oven for 30 minutes or until meat is richly browned and no longer pink when slashed. Drain briefly on paper towels and serve hot. Makes 4 servings.

ELEGANT CHAMPAGNE BUFFET features Creamy Scrambled Eggs (recipe at left) in Baked Potato Boats (page 79), with savory condiments of caviar, shrimp, blue-veined cheese, green onion slices, and bacon bits. Irresistible accompaniments are Marinated Mushroom Salad (page 77) and Banana Coffee Ring (page 66).

Brunch meats: Sausages, bacons & ham

Nothing perks up the appetite like the aroma of sausages browning atop the range, bacon crisping in the oven, or pan-fried ham slowly cooking until golden. All of these meats pair well with egg dishes, pancakes, waffles, and French toast. You can make a brunch as simple as a favorite meat accompanied by fruit or juice and warm buttery rolls. Or you can make it elaborate: stage a buffet laden with different varieties of cooked brunch meats, soft cheeses, an assortment of breads and rolls, and a basket full of fresh fruit of the season.

SAUSAGES

Sausages were among the first of the processed foods. Made of ground or chopped meat and seasonings, they were born out of the necessity to preserve meat without refrigeration. From its European beginnings 3,000 years ago, sausage-making has evolved into a worldwide industry producing over 200 different varieties.

In the 1800s, German and Austrian immigrants brought sausage-making to the United States. The "American hot dog," first served in 1904, was a type of sausage developed from their skills. Eventually, link sausages became a popular morning meat.

There are three main categories of sausages: country sausage, lightly cured sausage, and summer sausage (also known as "dry sausage").

Country sausage

Country sausage is raw when you buy it. It's made from raw ground meats (including pork) and is usually seasoned. It is sold in bulk, or stuffed into natural or manufactured casings and sold as links in every shape and size. Bratwurst, Italian, breakfast links, and pork sausage links are just a few examples.

These sausages are not vacuum sealed and are very perishable. You can find them in refrigerated sections of supermarkets, or purchase them over the meat counter. Store them in the refrigerator at 32°-40°F and use within 3 days. Or you can freeze them—they will keep for 1 month in the freezer before changing flavor.

Warning: *Never* taste raw pork (sometimes called "fresh pork"); even in this modern day there is danger of trichinosis. Because of this, your hands, cutting board, and cutting utensils should be thoroughly washed after you've handled raw pork. Country sausage, or any meat labeled "fresh pork," should be fully cooked to an internal temperature of 170°F or until it is no longer pink when slashed. Medium-low heat should be used for cooking links and patties to enable the heat to penetrate thoroughly and cook the sausages evenly; this minimizes shrinkage, too.

Purchase bulk country sausage by weight, not by the size or shape of the container. Figure about ¼ pound per person. Shape patties in 2½-inch rounds, ½ inch thick, and allow 2 per person. With links, the number you purchase and serve depends on their size; allow 2 or 3 small links per person, but only 1 per person of the larger links, such as Italian sausage or Bratwurst.

Cooking fresh links. Sausage links should never be pierced before or during cooking.

• *Baking:* Place links on a cold rack in a rimmed pan. Bake, uncovered and without turning, in a preheated 400° oven for 20 to 25 minutes or until links are no longer pink when slashed. Larger links may take an additional 10 minutes to bake.

• *Pan-frying:* For soft and lightly browned links, place sausages in a cold frying pan. Add 2 tablespoons water for every 4 links. Cover pan and bring just to simmering over medium heat. Reduce heat to low and simmer for 5 minutes. Drain off excess water. Cook, uncovered, over medium-low heat, shaking pan frequently, for 10 to 15 minutes or until sausages are browned on all sides.

Cooking patties. For even cooking, patties should be uniform in size—about ½ inch thick.

• *Baking:* Place patties on a cold rack in a rimmed pan. Bake, uncovered and without turning, in a preheated 400° oven for 20 to 25 minutes or until patties are no longer pink when slashed with a knife.

• *Pan-frying:* Place patties in a cold frying pan. Cook over medium-low heat for 7 to 10 minutes per side; drain on paper towels.

Lightly cured sausage

Lightly cured sausage, usually smoked and precooked, doesn't need cooking, but it tastes better if served warm. This category includes frankfurters, Vienna sausages, Polish sausages, and knockwurst. They will keep for a week in the refrigerator without changing flavor.

Summer sausage

Summer sausage (dry sausage) received its name because it was made during the winter and kept through the summer without refrigeration. Varieties of summer sausage include salami, pepperoni, and thuringer. Because of their thick protective casing and the added curing agents and preservatives, they keep for a long time. Once the casing has been broken, though, the meat will keep for only 2 to 3 weeks.

BACON & CANADIAN BACON

Bacon and Canadian bacon come from different cuts of pork. Regular bacon is from the pork side; Canadian bacon is from the pork loin that has been boned, rolled, cured, smoked, and fully cooked.

Freezing bacon is not recommended. The added preservatives redistribute throughout the meat at freezing temperatures, resulting in texture and flavor changes.

Allow 2 to 4 strips bacon per person, and about ⅛ to ¼ pound Canadian bacon per person.

Cooking bacon. To prevent curling and splattering, bacon should always be placed in a cold frying pan or on a cold rack.

• *Broiling:* Place separated bacon strips on rack in a rimmed pan. Broil about 6 inches from heat until done to your liking; turn once.

• *Baking:* Place separated bacon strips on rack in a rimmed pan. Bake, without turning, in a preheated 400° oven for about 10 minutes or until crisp.

• *Pan-frying:* Place bacon strips in frying pan over medium-low heat. Cook, turning 2 or 3 times for 8 to 10 minutes or until done to your liking; then drain.

Cooking Canadian bacon. For even cooking, cut all pieces ¼ inch thick and nick the edges every inch so bacon won't curl.

• *Broiling:* Place slices on a rack in a rimmed pan. Broil about 6 inches from heat in a preheated broiler for about 2 minutes per side.

• *Pan-frying:* Place slices in a lightly greased frying pan. Cook over medium-low heat for 2 or 3 minutes per side.

HAM

Hams are hind legs of pork that have been cured, then smoked and aged. They are labeled either "cook before eating" or "fully cooked." Whichever kind you purchase, the cooking instructions provided should be followed meticulously. The following are some general guidelines.

Hams labeled "cook before eating" are smoked and should be cooked in a 325° oven until the internal temperature reaches 170° on a meat thermometer. Cooking time varies for each cut of smoked ham. Cook a whole ham (10 to 14 lbs.) for 18 to 20 minutes per pound; cook a half (5 to 7 lbs.) for 22 to 25 minutes; cook a shank or butt end (3 to 4 lbs.) for 35 to 40 minutes.

Hams labeled "fully cooked" taste best if heated to an internal temperature of 140°. All canned hams are fully cooked; they are sterilized during the canning process. They can be kept refrigerated for 6 months in their purchased, unopened container. Once opened and sliced, they can be kept, refrigerated, for 3 to 5 days. Freezing is not recommended for ham; like bacon, it deteriorates in texture and flavor.

Boiled ham is trimmed, boneless ham that has been shaped into squares or rectangles, then cured and cooked. This is ready-to-eat meat.

Cooking smoked ham slice. Cut ham diagonally across the grain into a ¾ to 1-inch-thick slice. Nick edge fat at 1-inch intervals to prevent curling and splattering. You can brush the meat with a glaze during the last 4 minutes of cooking, if you wish. Serve ham alongside your entrée, or cut into serving pieces.

• *Broiling:* Place ham slice on a cold rack in a rimmed pan. Broil about 6 inches from heat in a preheated broiler, turning occasionally, for about 20 minutes.

• *Pan-frying:* Place ham slice in a lightly greased cold frying pan (do not add water). Cook over medium-low heat, turning occasionally, for about 20 minutes.

Spanish Eggs

Egg halves nestled in a tomato-vegetable sauce make a flavorful and colorful dish you can prepare the day before. Serve with warm, buttered tortillas.

        6 strips bacon
        1 cup *each* chopped green pepper and thinly sliced
           green onion
        ½ cup thinly sliced celery
        1 can (8 oz.) tomato sauce
        ¼ cup water
        1 can (2¼ oz.) sliced ripe olives, drained
        ½ teaspoon *each* dry basil and oregano leaves
        6 hard-cooked eggs (page 20), shelled and cut in half
           lengthwise

In a wide frying pan, over medium-high heat, cook bacon until crisp. Remove bacon from pan; drain, crumble, and set aside. Discard all but 2 tablespoons of the bacon drippings. To the drippings, add green pepper, onion, and celery; cook until onion is limp. Stir in tomato sauce and water; cook for 2 minutes or until heated through. Stir in olives, basil, oregano, and crumbled bacon; remove from heat. Pour mixture into a greased 1½-quart shallow baking dish. Arrange egg halves, cut side down, in tomato mixture, pushing down lightly to partially immerse eggs in sauce. (If made ahead, cool, cover, and refrigerate until next day.)

Bake, covered, in a 350° oven for 20 minutes (30 minutes, if refrigerated) or until heated through. Makes 4 to 6 servings.

Swiss Egg Ramekins

Onions, cooked slowly to sweetness, combine with Swiss cheese and a mild white sauce in this make-ahead egg entrée. Accompany with toasted English muffins and cherry tomatoes.

        3 tablespoons butter or margarine
        2 large onions, thinly sliced and separated into rings
        1 tablespoon all-purpose flour
        1 cup milk
        ½ teaspoon *each* Dijon mustard and salt
        2 teaspoons chopped parsley
        ⅛ teaspoon white pepper
        4 hard-cooked eggs (page 20), shelled and quartered
           lengthwise
     1½ cups (6 oz.) shredded Swiss cheese

In a wide frying pan over medium heat, melt 2 tablespoons of the butter. Add onions and cook slowly, uncovered, stirring often, until onion is limp and golden (about 30 minutes). Onions should not show signs of browning during first 15 minutes; if they do, reduce heat.

Meanwhile, melt the remaining 1 tablespoon butter in a 1-quart pan over medium heat. Stir in flour and cook until bubbly. Gradually stir in milk and cook, stirring constantly, until thick and smooth. Stir in mustard, salt, parsley, and pepper; set aside.

Divide onions evenly among four 10-ounce custard cups or ramekins (or assemble in a 1½-quart baking dish). Place four egg quarters, yolk side up, into each dish; equally distribute cheese, then white sauce, over eggs. (If made ahead, cool, cover, and refrigerate until next day.)

Bake, uncovered, in a 350° oven for about 30 minutes (40 minutes, if refrigerated) or until bubbly. Makes 4 servings.

Baja Soufflé Roll

Mexican cooks, renowned for their festive egg entrées, show off their expertise with this puffy, rolled soufflé. The airy egg mixture is baked in a jellyroll pan, then spread with sautéed onions and green chiles, and rolled up to be sliced.

Serve each slice crowned with avocado-sour cream sauce. Presented warm or at room temperature, it makes an impressive brunch entrée. Serve with fresh fruit of the season.

        2 tablespoons salad oil
        2 large onions, thinly sliced
        1 clove garlic, minced or pressed
        1 can (7 oz.) diced green chiles
        ½ cup all-purpose flour
        2 cups milk
        ¼ teaspoon *each* salt and ground cumin
        ⅛ teaspoon pepper
        4 eggs, separated
        ½ cup shredded jack cheese
        1 teaspoon sugar
           Avocado sauce (directions follow)
           Pitted ripe olives

In a wide frying pan over medium heat, add oil. When oil is hot, add onion and garlic and cook until onion is limp. Stir in chiles, then set aside.

Line a greased 10 by 15-inch jellyroll pan with foil. Butter foil generously, then dust with flour; shake out excess flour and set pan aside.

Place the ½ cup flour in a 2 or 3-quart pan. Very gradually add milk, stirring constantly with a wire whip until smooth. Stir in salt, cumin, and pepper.

(Continued on next page)

EHOLD THE SOUFFLÉ—the aristocrat
f the egg family, but remarkably simple to make.
his billowy, flavorful Spinach Soufflé makes a
rand entrée for six. The recipe is on page 33.

Place over medium heat and cook, stirring, until thickened. Lightly beat egg yolks, then beat in several spoonfuls of the heated sauce. Stir egg yolk mixture back into sauce, add cheese and cook, stirring, for 1 minute; set aside.

Beat egg whites until foamy; add sugar and beat until moist, stiff peaks form. Gently fold sauce into beaten whites just until blended. Pour mixture into prepared jellyroll pan and spread evenly. Bake in a preheated 325° oven for 40 to 45 minutes or until golden brown and puffy.

Immediately turn soufflé out onto a wax paper-covered baking sheet; carefully remove foil. Spread onion mixture evenly over soufflé. Using the wax paper as support, roll soufflé into a compact cylinder. To serve, cut roll into thick slices; pass avocado sauce to spoon over individual servings. Garnish with olives. Makes about 6 servings.

Avocado sauce. Peel, pit, and mash 1 medium-size **avocado.** Stir in 2 tablespoons *each* **lime juice** and chopped **green onion;** 1 **clove garlic,** minced or pressed; ⅓ cup **sour cream;** ¼ teaspoon ground **cumin;** and **salt** and **pepper** to taste.

Tuna Soufflé

Here's an attractive tuna entrée that can be assembled in minutes with ingredients you usually have on hand. You should be ready to sit down and eat as soon as it is out of the oven. Fresh fruit and crusty rolls are good accompaniments.

- 3 **tablespoons butter or margarine**
- 3 **tablespoons all-purpose flour**
- 1 **cup milk**
- 1 **can (about 7 oz.) chunk-style tuna, drained and flaked**
- ½ **teaspoon** *each* **salt and paprika**
- 2 **tablespoons chopped chives or green onions**
- 4 **eggs**
  Cheese sauce (directions follow)

Preheat oven to 350°. In a pan over medium heat, melt butter. Stir in flour and cook until bubbly. Gradually stir in milk; cook, stirring constantly, until thickened. Add tuna, salt, paprika, and chives; continue to cook and stir until hot. Remove from heat; cool slightly.

While sauce cools, carefully separate eggs. Beat 2 yolks at a time into sauce mixture.

In a large bowl, beat egg whites with clean beaters just until stiff, moist peaks form. Carefully fold about ¼ of the beaten whites into sauce mixture; then pour mixture over remaining egg whites and gently fold together.

Pour into a well-buttered 1½-quart soufflé dish. Bake in the preheated 350° oven for 35 to 40 minutes or until top is golden and puffy and center is firm when touched. Prepare cheese sauce while soufflé bakes. Serve soufflé immediately. Spoon some sauce over each serving. Makes 4 or 5 servings.

Cheese sauce. In a pan over medium heat, melt 1 tablespoon **butter** or margarine. Stir in 1 tablespoon all-purpose **flour** and ¼ teaspoon *each* **salt, paprika, and dry mustard;** cook until bubbly. Gradually stir in 1 cup **milk** and cook, stirring constantly, until thickened. Stir in ½ cup shredded **Swiss or jack cheese** until melted.

Egg & Cheese Ramekins

These individual egg puffs rise dramatically like soufflés, but they are much easier to make: simply beat eggs and bake with cheese. You'll want your table completely ready and your guests seated before the eggs are done, though, because the puffs fall quickly after coming out of the oven.

- 1½ **cups (6 oz.) shredded sharp Cheddar cheese**
- 6 **eggs**
- ½ **cup half-and-half (light cream)**
- 3 **tablespoons all-purpose flour**
- 1½ **teaspoons dry mustard**
- ¼ **teaspoon** *each* **salt and pepper**

Preheat oven to 325°. Evenly distribute cheese into 4 well-buttered 10-ounce soufflé dishes or custard cups. With a rotary beater, beat together eggs, half-and-half, flour, mustard, salt, and pepper. Pour equal amounts of the egg mixture into each dish. Place dishes on a baking sheet and bake for 35 to 40 minutes or until tops are golden and puffy. Serve immediately. Makes 4 servings.

Chile-Egg Puff

Quick-to-make Mexican-style baked eggs are an excellent buffet choice. For a more intimate group, cut the recipe in half and pour into an 8-inch-square baking pan. Accompany with fried ham slices.

- 10 **eggs**
- ½ **cup all-purpose flour**
- 1 **teaspoon baking powder**
- ½ **teaspoon salt**
- 2 **cups (16 oz.) cottage cheese**
- 4 **cups (1 lb.) shredded jack cheese**
- ½ **cup butter or margarine, melted and cooled**
- 2 **cans (4 oz.** *each***) diced green chiles**

Preheat oven to 350°. In a medium-size bowl, beat eggs until light and lemon colored. Add flour, baking powder, salt, cottage cheese, jack cheese, and butter; blend until smooth. Stir in chiles.

Pour mixture into a well-buttered 9 by 13-inch baking pan. Bake in the preheated 350° oven for about 35 minutes or until top is browned and center appears firm. Serve immediately. Makes 10 to 12 servings.

Spinach Soufflé

(Pictured on page 30)

Canned cream of chicken soup gives extra stability to a light spinach soufflé. Serve this speedy entrée with hot buttered rolls and fresh fruit.

- 1 can (about 10¾ oz.) condensed cream of chicken soup
- ½ cup *each* shredded Cheddar and jack cheeses
- 1 teaspoon dry mustard
- ¼ teaspoon ground nutmeg
- 6 eggs
- 1 package (10 or 12 oz.) frozen chopped spinach, thawed
- ¼ cup finely chopped green onion, including some tops
- 2 teaspoons lemon juice

Preheat oven to 375°. In a pan, combine soup, Cheddar and jack cheeses, mustard, and nutmeg. Cook over low heat, stirring frequently, until cheese melts. Remove from heat and cool slightly.

While sauce cools, carefully separate eggs. Beat yolks 2 at a time into soup mixture. Squeeze out any

excess liquid from spinach. Add spinach, onions, and lemon juice to soup mixture; stir to blend.

In a large bowl, beat egg whites with clean beaters just until stiff, moist peaks form. Carefully fold about ¼ of the beaten whites into soup mixture; then pour mixture over egg whites and gently fold together.

Pour into a well-buttered 2-quart soufflé dish or straight-sided deep 2-quart baking dish. Bake in the preheated 375° oven for 30 to 35 minutes or until center feels firm when touched and jiggles only slightly when gently shaken. Serve immediately. Makes 6 servings.

Asparagus Cheese Strata

This layered asparagus, cheese, and ham bake is a good choice to serve buffet-style because you can assemble it completely the day before, then cover and refrigerate it overnight. It cuts so easily, you can serve it in nice neat squares.

- 1 pound fresh asparagus or 2 packages (9 oz. *each*) frozen asparagus pieces
  Boiling, salted water
- 6 slices whole wheat bread
  Butter or margarine
- 2¼ cups (9 oz.) shredded Cheddar cheese
- 1 cup coarsely chopped cooked ham
- 5 eggs
- 2 tablespoons instant minced onion
- ¾ teaspoon *each* dry mustard and Worcestershire
- ¼ teaspoon *each* salt and garlic powder
  Dash of cayenne
- 1¾ cups milk

Remove tough ends from fresh asparagus and cut diagonally into 1-inch pieces. Drop into boiling salted water to cover; cook rapidly just until tender (about 4 minutes). Lift from pan with slotted spoon, drain, and set aside. (If using frozen asparagus, cook as directed on package; drain and set aside.)

Trim crusts from bread. Butter slices lightly and fit into a lightly buttered 7 by 11-inch baking dish. Sprinkle 1½ cups of the cheese over bread slices. Top with ham and asparagus pieces in even layers.

In a bowl, stir together eggs, onion, mustard, Worcestershire, salt, garlic powder, and cayenne. Add milk and beat together until mixture is well blended. Pour evenly over layered ingredients. Cover and refrigerate for at least 8 hours or overnight.

Bake, uncovered, in a 350° oven for 30 minutes; then top with the remaining ¾ cup cheese. Bake for an additional 10 minutes or until center of strata appears firm when dish is gently shaken. Let stand for 5 minutes before cutting into squares. Makes 6 to 8 servings.

Individual Omelets

(Pictured on opposite page)

Once you know how, you can turn out individual omelets for three or four people in only a few minutes — and the technique isn't difficult to master. You'll need an omelet pan or any fairly heavy frying pan with sloping sides. A 7 or 8-inch-diameter pan is recommended for the two or three-egg omelet this recipe makes. Several suggestions for fillings are given below; but the choices are endless.

    2 or 3 eggs
    ¼ teaspoon salt
      Dash of pepper
    1 tablespoon water
    ½ to 1 tablespoon butter or margarine
      Fillings (suggestions follow)

For each individual omelet, break eggs into a small bowl and add salt, pepper, and water. Beat just enough to mix yolks and whites.

Heat an omelet pan (or a 7 or 8-inch frying pan with sloping sides) over medium-high heat; melt butter, and tilt pan to coat bottom and sides. Pour in egg mixture and cook, gently lifting cooked portion to allow uncooked portion to flow underneath. Gently shake pan to keep omelet free. Continue to shake pan and lift omelet edges until there is no more liquid but the top still looks moist and creamy.

Spoon 2 or 3 tablespoons filling down center of omelet, in line with pan handle. Fold omelet in thirds according to directions on page 21. Makes 1 serving.

Fillings. Use alone or in combination: **shredded cheese** (jack, Cheddar or Parmesan); thinly sliced **spinach leaves;** diced **avocado;** sliced **mushrooms** (raw or sautéed in butter); **bacon bits;** diced **salami** or ham; diced **tomato;** small **shrimp; jelly; sour cream; lox; cream cheese;** or **sprouts.**

Bacon & Tomato Omelet

Here is a delicious combination of bacon, eggs, cheese, and tomatoes all cooked together into a big omelet. Cut in wedges and serve directly from the frying pan. Accompany with chilled fruit juice and sweet mini-muffins (page 63).

    1 large tomato
    6 eggs
    ½ teaspoon *each* salt and dry basil
    ¼ teaspoon pepper
    2 tablespoons finely chopped parsley
    4 to 8 strips bacon
    1 medium-size onion, chopped
    1 cup (4 oz.) shredded Cheddar cheese

Peel tomato, cut in half, and squeeze gently to remove some of the seeds. Cut halves into thin slices and set aside. In a bowl, mix eggs, salt, basil, pepper, and parsley; set aside.

In a 10-inch frying pan, cook bacon until crisp. Remove bacon from pan, drain, crumble, and set aside. Discard all but 2 tablespoons of the bacon drippings from pan.

Place frying pan with 2 tablespoons drippings over medium-high heat; add onion and cook, stirring often, until soft (about 3 to 5 minutes). Distribute tomato slices in a single layer over onion; cook for about 1 minute, then sprinkle cheese over tomatoes. Pour egg mixture into pan and tilt pan so eggs flow evenly around tomatoes. Cook just until bottom layer of egg is set (about 2 minutes). Place pan in preheated broiler about 6 inches from heat until eggs are set on top (2 to 3 minutes). Sprinkle crumbled bacon on top of omelet and serve at once. Makes 4 or 5 servings.

Basil Frittata with Italian Sausages in Pepper Sauce

A frittata is an Italian omelet made with eggs and vegetables that are often stirred together before cooking. This basil-flavored frittata is served with a fresh-tasting sauce of bell peppers, tomatoes, and mild sausages.

      Italian sausages in pepper sauce (directions
        follow)
    ¾ cup sour cream
    12 eggs
    ¾ teaspoon salt
    ¼ teaspoon pepper
    2 tablespoons finely chopped fresh basil or 2
        teaspoons dry basil
    3 tablespoons butter or margarine
    ½ cup thinly sliced green onion
    ⅔ cup (3 oz.) freshly grated Parmesan cheese

Brown sausages and make pepper sauce; cover and refrigerate if made ahead.

Place sour cream in a bowl; beat in eggs, one at a time. Stir in salt, pepper, and basil; set aside.

In a 10-inch frying pan with ovenproof handle, melt 2 tablespoons of the butter over medium heat. Add onion and cook, stirring, for 1 minute. Pour in

(Continued on page 36)

STAGE AN OMELET PARTY in front of the fire. To enfold in Individual Omelets (recipe at left), offer Carrot & Zucchini Medley (page 77) and an array of other fillings and toppings: sautéed mushrooms, shredded jack and Cheddar cheeses, jelly, sour cream, sweet onion slices, whipped cream cheese, crumbled bacon, smoked salmon, chunks of tomato and avocado, and sprouts. For compatible partners, a tray of beautiful breads and a big pitcher of iced orange juice.

egg mixture. Cook, lifting set portion of frittata with a spatula to allow uncooked portion to flow underneath. Continue cooking until eggs are softly set but the top still looks moist and creamy. Remove from heat; sprinkle with cheese. Place in preheated broiler about 6 inches from heat just until cheese melts. Cut into wedges to serve warm with sausages and pepper sauce. Makes about 6 servings.

Italian sausages in pepper sauce. In a 12-inch frying pan (or Dutch oven) over medium heat, cook 6 to 8 **mild Italian sausages** (about 1¼ lbs.) until well browned; remove from pan and set aside. Measure drippings and add enough **salad oil** to make 4 tablespoons total; add to pan with 1 large **onion,** chopped, and 1 clove **garlic,** minced or pressed. Cook, stirring frequently, until limp. Add 5 medium-size **red or green bell peppers,** seeded and cut into ½-inch strips; cook, stirring, for 3 minutes. Add 4 cups (2½ lbs.) peeled, seeded, and chopped **tomatoes;** ⅓ cup finely chopped **fresh basil** or 1½ tablespoons dry basil; 1¼ teaspoons **salt;** and 1 tablespoon **sugar.** Mix 1 teaspoon **cornstarch** with 1 teaspoon **water** and stir into sauce. Bring to a boil, stirring constantly, until most of the liquid has evaporated.

Place sausages on top of the sauce, cover, and keep warm while making the frittata. (If made ahead, cool, cover, and refrigerate until next day to reheat while frittata is cooking.)

Sour Cream & Ham Oven Omelet

You start cooking this puffy omelet on top of the range and then put it in the oven to bake. The omelet goes together quickly if you separate the eggs, dice

the ham, and chop the parsley and onions ahead. Serve with glazed apples or pears (page 4).

> 5 **eggs, separated**
> ½ cup **sour cream**
> 3 tablespoons *each* chopped **parsley and green onion**
> 1 cup finely diced cooked **ham**
> 1½ tablespoons **butter** or margarine
> **Sour cream**

In a large bowl, beat egg whites until stiff, moist peaks form. In another bowl, beat egg yolks until very thick. Beat sour cream into yolks, then stir in parsley, onion, and ham. Pour yolk mixture over beaten whites and gently fold together.

In an omelet pan (or a 10-inch frying pan with sloping sides and ovenproof handle), melt butter over medium heat. Tilt pan so butter coats bottom and sides of pan. Pour omelet mixture into pan and smooth surface gently for even cooking. Reduce heat to low and cook until edges are lightly browned (about 7 to 10 minutes); lift edge of omelet with a spatula to test.

Place pan in a 325° oven and bake for 12 to 15 minutes or until a knife inserted in center comes out clean.

Run a spatula around edge of omelet, then tip pan and slide spatula under omelet to loosen from pan. Slide omelet out onto a warm serving plate. Separate into wedges with two forks or gently cut with a knife. Serve with additional sour cream. Makes about 4 servings.

Potato Omelet

Crusty potatoes and garlic abound in this range-top omelet you can serve right from the pan. We give a range of garlic for this recipe; use only the amount that suits your taste. You could start by trying the lesser amount and using more the next time.

> ¼ cup **olive oil** or salad oil
> 2 medium-size **potatoes** (about 1 lb. total), cut into ½-inch cubes
> 1 cup chopped **green onion,** including tops
> ¼ cup finely chopped **parsley**
> 2 to 4 cloves **garlic,** minced or pressed
> 6 **eggs**
> ¼ cup **milk**
> ½ teaspoon **salt**
> ⅛ teaspoon **pepper**
> Prepared **salsa** or taco sauce (optional)

In a wide frying pan, heat oil over medium-high heat; add potatoes and cook, stirring, until golden (about 15 minutes). Add onion, parsley, and garlic; cook, stirring, until onion is limp and potatoes are crusty brown. Reduce heat and distribute potato mixture evenly over bottom of pan.

Lightly beat eggs and milk together; stir in salt and pepper. Pour egg mixture evenly over potato mixture and cook, uncovered, for 5 to 7 minutes or until eggs are set on the bottom. Run a spatula around edge of omelet and slide spatula underneath omelet to loosen from pan. Cover, remove from heat, and let stand just until top is set (about 5 minutes).

Cut into wedges. Pass salsa at the table, if desired. Makes 4 servings.

Sweet Puffy Omelet

Impressive when served right from the oven, this sugar-coated baked omelet deflates quickly, so have everyone seated at the table and ready to eat. Serve with sausages or ham slices, crunchy bran muffins, and melon wedges.

  3 tablespoons butter or margarine
  ¼ cup sifted powdered sugar
  2 tablespoons whipping cream
  6 eggs, separated
  ⅛ teaspoon salt
  2 tablespoons granulated sugar
  2 teaspoons grated orange peel
     Cherry or strawberry preserves (optional)

In an 8 by 12-inch baking pan, melt butter in a 375° oven; add 2 tablespoons of the powdered sugar along with cream and stir to blend; set aside.

In a large bowl, beat egg whites with salt until soft peaks form; gradually add granulated sugar and beat until stiff. In another bowl, beat egg yolks until thick; mix in grated orange peel. Pour yolks over egg whites and gently fold together. Spoon into the baking pan and swirl top with spoon. Shake the remaining 2 tablespoons powdered sugar through a wire strainer over top.

Bake in the preheated 375° oven for 12 to 14 minutes or until top is golden brown. Serve at once. Pass cherry or strawberry preserves to spoon over top, if desired. Makes 4 to 6 servings.

Crustless Bacon & Cheese Quiche

This cheese-filled, crustless quiche is easy to assemble and cuts neatly into wedges or squares for individual servings. Any remaining quiche can be reheated the following day.

  1 pound sliced bacon
     About 4 medium-size leeks
 10 eggs
  2 cups milk
  ½ teaspoon salt
  ⅛ teaspoon ground nutmeg
  3 cups (12 oz.) shredded Swiss cheese
  ¼ pound sliced cooked ham, cut in strips

Cut bacon in 1-inch pieces and cook in a wide frying pan over medium heat until crisp. Remove from pan with a slotted spoon and drain on paper towels. Discard all but 2 tablespoons bacon drippings.

Cut leeks in half lengthwise and wash thoroughly. Thinly slice white part of leeks and about 2 inches of the green part; add to bacon drippings and cook until leeks are limp.

In a bowl, lightly beat eggs until blended; stir in milk, salt, and nutmeg. Reserve ¼ cup *each* of the bacon and cheese for the top; add remaining cheese and bacon to egg mixture along with leeks and ham. Turn into a greased 2-quart baking dish. Sprinkle reserved cheese and bacon on top. Bake, uncovered, in 350° oven for 35 to 40 minutes or until a knife inserted in center comes out clean. Let stand for 10 minutes before serving. Makes 6 to 8 servings.

Crab Quiche

Warm crab quiche, dotted with red pimentos and green onions, is quick to make and colorful to serve. If crab isn't in season, substitute a can of tuna.

  9-inch unbaked pastry shell, 1½ inches deep
  ½ pound crab meat or 1 large can (about 9 oz.) chunk-style tuna (drained and flaked)
  1 cup (4 oz.) shredded Swiss cheese
  ¼ cup *each* grated Parmesan cheese and chopped green onion (tops included)
  1 jar (2 oz.) diced pimento, drained
  3 eggs
  1 cup milk
  ½ teaspoon salt
  ¼ teaspoon ground nutmeg
  ⅛ teaspoon pepper

Bake pastry shell in a preheated 450° oven for 7 to 10 minutes or until crust is lightly browned. Remove from oven and reduce oven temperature to 350°.

Distribute crab evenly over bottom of baked pastry shell. Evenly layer Swiss cheese, Parmesan cheese, onion, and pimento on top.

In a bowl, lightly beat eggs; stir in milk, salt, nutmeg, and pepper; pour over crab and cheese. Bake in a 350° oven for about 45 minutes or until a knife inserted in center comes out clean. Let stand for 10 minutes before cutting. Makes 4 to 6 servings.

Mushroom Crust Quiche

Sautéed mushrooms form the crust for an elegant baked cheese custard pie. Serve this savory quiche with a fruit compote and sweet rolls.

  5 tablespoons butter or margarine
  ½ pound mushrooms, coarsely chopped
  ½ cup finely crushed saltine crackers
  ¾ cup chopped green onion
  2 cups (8 oz.) shredded jack or Swiss cheese
  1 cup cottage cheese
  3 eggs
  ¼ teaspoon *each* cayenne and paprika

In a frying pan over medium heat, melt 3 tablespoons of the butter; add mushrooms and cook until limp. Stir in crushed crackers, then turn mixture into a well-greased 9-inch pie pan. Press mixture evenly over pan bottom and up the sides.

In same frying pan over medium heat, melt remaining 2 tablespoons butter; add onion, and cook until limp. Spread onions over mushroom crust; sprinkle evenly with shredded cheese. In a blender, whirl cottage cheese, eggs, and cayenne until smooth. Pour into crust and sprinkle with paprika. Bake in a 350° oven for about 20 to 25 minutes or until a knife inserted just off center comes out clean. Let stand for 10 to 15 minutes before cutting. Makes 4 to 6 servings.

Individual Cheese Quiches

(Pictured on opposite page)

Laced with crisp, crumbled bacon and cheese, these individual quiches make great eat-out-of-hand picnic fare.

1½ cups all-purpose flour
  ¼ teaspoon salt
 10 tablespoons (¼ lb. plus 2 tablespoons) butter or
       margarine
  3 eggs
 10 strips bacon, cooked, drained, and crumbled
  1 cup (4 oz.) shredded Swiss or Gruyère cheese
1½ cups half-and-half (light cream)
       Dash of pepper
       Chopped parsley

In a bowl, combine flour and salt. Cut butter into chunks and add to flour mixture. With two knives or

a pastry blender, cut butter into flour until you have fine particles. Add 1 of the eggs and stir with a fork until dough holds together. Shape dough into a ball. If made ahead, cover and refrigerate; bring to room temperature before continuing.

Divide dough evenly among eight 4-inch tart pans (or ten 3-inch pans). Press dough evenly over bottom and sides of pans.

Set pans on a baking sheet. Evenly distribute bacon among pastry shells, then evenly distribute cheese over bacon.

In a small bowl, beat remaining 2 eggs with half-and-half and pepper. Divide egg mixture equally among pastry shells (don't let mixture overflow or pastry will stick). Sprinkle each with parsley.

Set baking sheet on lowest rack in a 350° oven. Bake for 35 to 40 minutes or until filling puffs (it settles when cooled) and tops are lightly browned. Let stand for about 10 minutes; then, protecting your hands, tip each quiche out of its pan into your hand and place, filling side up, on a rack to cool further. If made ahead, cool completely, cover, and refrigerate. To serve, bring to room temperature or reheat by placing quiches, side by side, on a baking sheet in a 350° oven for 10 minutes. Makes 8 quiches 4-inch size, or 10 quiches 3-inch size.

Shrimp-Olive Quiche

Cheese, shrimp, and sliced olives bake in this savory custard seasoned with shrimp soup. Serve it with slices of avocado and tomatoes.

  9 - inch unbaked pastry shell, 1½ inches deep
  2 cups (8 oz.) shredded jack cheese
  ½ pound small cooked shrimp
  1 can (2¼ oz.) sliced ripe olives, drained
  3 eggs
  1 can (about 10¾ oz.) condensed cream of
       shrimp soup
  ⅓ cup milk
  ¼ teaspoon *each* onion and garlic powder
       About 4 drops liquid hot pepper seasoning
       Paprika

Bake pastry shell in a preheated 450° oven for 7 to 10 minutes or until crust is lightly browned. Remove from oven and reduce oven temperature to 375°. Layer cheese, shrimp, and olives in pastry shell.

In a bowl, lightly beat eggs; stir in soup, milk, onion and garlic powders, and hot pepper seasoning. Pour over olives and sprinkle with paprika.

Bake in the preheated 375° oven for about 40 minutes or until a knife inserted in center comes out clean. Let stand for 10 minutes before cutting. Makes 4 to 6 servings.

Pancakes & Waffles

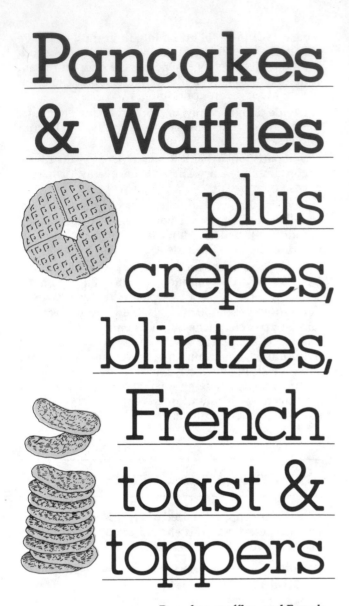

plus crêpes, blintzes, French toast & toppers

Pancakes, waffles, and French toast are always a bonus. They're quick enough to satisfy a weekday morning whim, yet special enough to gratify the weekend wish for a leisurely, elaborate brunch. Some are light and airy, others are quite substantial and hearty.

In this chapter, we offer recipes for such festive refections as Mexican-tamale pancakes, tender feathery crêpes loaded with savory fillings, and sour cream waffles topped with a creamy shrimp and mushroom sauce. Others, like our freezer French toast, old-fashioned oatmeal pancakes, and basic pancakes and waffles, acquire a festive air when generously topped with one of our quick and easy homemade syrups, sauces, or flavored butters.

Buttermilk & Sherry Hotcakes

Tender, light, and golden are the words that best describe these little melt-in-your-mouth pancakes. The sherry gives them an added touch of sweetness; cooking them in melted butter or margarine prevents sticking and gives them a nice golden color. Sprinkle with powdered sugar and melted butter and serve with your favorite jam.

  1 egg, separated
 ¾ cup buttermilk
  1 tablespoon salad oil
  2 tablespoons cream sherry
 ⅔ cup all-purpose flour
  2 tablespoons cornmeal
 ½ teaspoon *each* baking powder and soda
 ¼ teaspoon salt
     Butter or margarine

In a medium-size bowl, beat egg white just until stiff, moist peaks form. In a large bowl, beat egg yolk, buttermilk, oil, and sherry together until frothy; then blend in flour, cornmeal, baking powder, soda, and salt. Fold beaten white into buttermilk mixture.

Preheat a griddle or large frying pan over medium heat; when hot, melt enough butter to coat cooking surface. Spoon batter, about 3 tablespoons for each cake, onto griddle; spread batter to make 3-inch circles. Cook until tops are bubbly and appear dry; turn and cook other sides until browned. Add butter as needed. Makes about 1 dozen pancakes.

Cottage Cheese Pancakes with Applesauce

These pancakes are not only light and moist, they're even high in protein. To save clean-up time, whirl the ingredients in a blender and pour batter directly onto a hot greased griddle. Use either homemade or canned applesauce (you can blend a few dashes of ground cinnamon and nutmeg directly into canned applesauce, if you prefer added spice). Serve with browned sausage patties.

  3 eggs
  1 cup small-curd cottage cheese
  2 tablespoons salad oil
 ¼ cup all-purpose flour
 ¼ teaspoon salt
  1 cup applesauce
     Powdered sugar
     Ground cinnamon
     Sour cream (optional)

Break eggs into blender or food processor container. Add cottage cheese and whirl until blended. Add oil, flour, and salt; whirl until mixture is almost smooth. Preheat a griddle or large frying pan over medium heat; grease lightly. Pour batter, about ¼ cup for each cake, onto griddle. Cook until tops are bubbly and appear dry; turn and cook other sides until browned.

While pancakes are cooking, heat applesauce in a small pan over medium heat until heated through. Spoon 1 or 2 tablespoons of warm applesauce down center of each pancake and roll to enclose. Sprinkle each filled pancake with sifted powdered sugar and cinnamon. Pass sour cream at the table to spoon atop pancakes, if desired. Makes about 8 pancakes.

Mexican Tamale Pancakes

Robust is the word for these spicy cornmeal pancakes studded with golden corn and ripe olives. They may sound a little offbeat, but once you've tried them you'll want to make them again. Pass bowls of shredded cheese, chopped tomatoes, onions, sour cream, and taco sauce to embellish the pancakes. Serve with crisp bacon strips, browned sausages or pan-fried chorizo. If you add freshly squeezed fruit juice or a fresh fruit compote to the menu you'll have a hearty brunch.

  1 **cup yellow cornmeal**
  1 **cup boiling water**
  1 **cup milk**
  ⅓ **cup salad oil**
  1 **egg, well beaten**
  1 **cup baking mix (biscuit mix)**
  1 **teaspoon** *each* **salt and ground cumin**
  ½ **teaspoon chili powder**
  2 **teaspoons baking powder**
  1 **can (about 8 oz.) whole kernel corn, well drained**
  1 **can (4½ oz.) chopped ripe olives, well drained**
     Condiments: 1 to 1½ cups *each* **shredded Cheddar cheese, chopped green onion (including tops), chopped tomatoes, sour cream, and prepared taco sauce.**

Put cornmeal in a medium-size bowl. Pour boiling water over cornmeal and stir well; let cool for about 10 minutes. Add milk, oil, and egg; mix until well blended. Add baking mix, salt, cumin, chili powder, and baking powder; beat until smooth. Stir in corn and olives.

Preheat a griddle or large frying pan over medium heat; grease well. Spoon batter, about 3 tablespoons for each cake, onto griddle; spread batter to make 4-inch circles. Cook until tops are bubbly and appear dry; turn and cook other sides until browned. At the table, pass individual bowls of condiments. Makes about 2 dozen pancakes.

Old-fashioned Oatmeal Pancakes

Start the batter for these moist, cakelike pancakes the night before. Finish the next day, bake the pancakes, and serve with syrup, jam, or flavored butter (page 52). Serve with crisp bacon strips alongside.

  2 **cups** *each* **regular rolled oats and buttermilk**
  2 **eggs, lightly beaten**
  ¼ **cup butter or margarine, melted and cooled**
  ½ **cup raisins (optional)**
  ½ **cup all-purpose flour**
  2 **tablespoons sugar**
  1 **teaspoon** *each* **baking powder and soda**
  ½ **teaspoon ground cinnamon**
  ¼ **teaspoon salt**

In a bowl, combine oats and buttermilk; stir to blend well. Cover and refrigerate until next day.

Just before cooking, add eggs, butter, and raisins (if desired); stir just to blend. In another bowl, stir together flour, sugar, baking powder, soda, cinnamon, and salt; add to oat mixture and stir just until moistened. If batter seems too thick, add more buttermilk (up to 3 tablespoons).

Preheat a griddle or large frying pan over medium heat; grease lightly. Spoon batter, about ⅓ cup for each cake, onto griddle; spread batter out to make 4-inch circles. Cook until tops are bubbly and appear dry; turn and cook other sides until browned. Makes about 1½ dozen pancakes.

Finnish Pancake

Like many other dairy-rich dishes typical of the western provinces of Finland, this billowy, custardlike oven pancake is a tempting blend of butter, eggs, milk, and honey. Serve it right away—it falls as it cools. Top with fresh fruit of the season and drizzle with more honey, or your favorite topping.

  4 **eggs**
  ¼ **cup honey**
  ¾ **teaspoon salt**
2½ **cups milk**
  1 **cup all-purpose flour**
  4 **tablespoons butter or margarine**

Preheat a heavy frying pan (about 10 inches wide by 3 inches deep) with an ovenproof handle in a 425° oven for about 10 minutes.

Meanwhile, in a bowl, beat together eggs, honey, salt, and milk. Add flour; beat until blended and smooth.

(Continued on next page)

Remove pan from oven, melt butter in pan, then add batter. Return pan to oven and bake for about 25 minutes, or until a knife inserted in center of pancake comes out clean. Serve immediately. Makes 4 to 6 servings.

Aebleskiver *(Danish Pancake Balls)*

(Pictured on opposite page)

The tender ball-shaped pancakes the Danish call "aebleskiver" derive their roundness from the iron in which they're cooked. This specialty iron can be bought in gourmet cookware shops or in department store housewares sections.

To make perfectly round aebleskiver, you must frequently lift and turn the baked section of each ball. They will eventually seal themselves, creating a hollow in each center. Serve with your favorite jam or preserves.

1¼ cups all-purpose flour
½ teaspoon salt
2¼ teaspoons baking powder
2 tablespoons granulated sugar
½ teaspoon ground cardamom or ground cinnamon
1 egg, beaten
1 cup milk
About 3 tablespoons butter or margarine, melted and cooled
Powdered sugar
Fruit jam or preserves

In a medium-size bowl, sift flour with salt, baking powder, granulated sugar, and cardamom. In a small bowl, combine egg, milk, and 2 tablespoons of the butter; add to flour mixture and stir until blended and smooth.

Place a seasoned (page 57) aebleskiver pan over medium heat until water sprinkled in pan sizzles. Brush each cup lightly with some of the remaining butter. Fill each cup about 2/3 full with batter. In about 30 seconds, a thin shell forms on the bottom of each pancake ball. Stick a slender wooden or metal skewer into baked portion and gently pull shell almost halfway up, so unbaked batter flows out.

Continue to rotate each pancake ball about every 30 seconds as the shell begins to set, pulling up the baked shell to let remaining batter flow out into cup. After about four turns, the ball should be almost formed and you can turn it upside down to seal. Continue baking, rotating the balls frequently until they are an even golden brown and a skewer inserted in center comes out clean. With skewer, lift balls from pan when baked. Repeat with remaining batter.

Serve immediately, or keep warm for as long as 30 minutes in a bun warmer or cloth-lined basket on an electric warming tray. When ready to serve, dust with powdered sugar. Break each ball in half, fill with jam, and eat out-of-hand. Makes 12 to 15 pancake balls.

Walnut-Wheat Griddle Cakes

Soy flour and whole wheat flour combine with walnuts in this recipe to produce tender, moist, crunchy pancakes. This batter spreads out, so leave plenty of room on the griddle between poured pancakes. Offer hot pineapple sauce (page 53), bacon strips or sausages, and a fresh fruit tray to complete the menu.

2 cups whole wheat flour
⅔ cup soy flour
1½ teaspoons salt
6 teaspoons baking powder
4 eggs, lightly beaten
2½ cups milk
¼ cup honey
⅔ cup salad oil
1 cup chopped walnuts

In a large bowl, stir together whole wheat flour, soy flour, salt, and baking powder; blend well. In a medium-size bowl, combine eggs, milk, honey, and oil; pour all at once into flour mixture and stir until smooth. Stir in nuts.

Preheat a griddle or large frying pan over medium heat; grease lightly. Pour batter, about ¼ cup, onto griddle to make 4-inch circles; space them well apart (they spread). Cook until tops are bubbly and appear dry; turn and cook other sides until browned. Makes 2 to 2½ dozen pancakes.

Pigs-in-a-Blanket

Tender cornmeal pancakes wrapped around browned sausage links are sure to be a favorite with children. They are easy to eat out of hand and make great backyard picnic fare with bananas, orange wedges, and cold glasses of milk.

1⅓ cups baking mix (biscuit mix)
½ cup yellow cornmeal
1 cup milk
2 eggs, lightly beaten
2 tablespoons salad oil
12 precooked sausage links

(Continued on page 44)

THE DANES CALL THEM AEBLESKIVER, these golden, puffy pancake balls that make a sweet morning treat when broken in half and filled with your favorite jam. The recipe is at left.

In a large bowl, combine baking mix and cornmeal. Stir together milk, eggs, and oil; pour all at once into corn meal mixture and stir just until blended.

Preheat a griddle or large frying pan over medium heat; grease lightly. Pour batter, about ¼ cup at a time, onto griddle to make 4-inch circles. Cook until tops are bubbly and appear dry; turn and cook other sides until browned. Remove to an ovenproof plat-ter. Cover and keep warm in a 200° oven until all pancakes have been made.

While pancakes are cooking, prepare sausages. In a wide frying pan over medium heat, brown sausages well on all sides. Cover and keep warm until all pancakes have been cooked.

Place one sausage in center of each pancake and roll to enclose. Makes 12 pigs-in-a-blanket.

Spectacular, easy & delicious: Big Dutch babies

(Pictured on page 46)

This recipe originated at Manca's, a family-run restaurant that was practically an institution in Seattle during the first half of this century. Victor Manca made oven miniatures of a big German pancake. His children dubbed them "Dutch babies" and the name stuck. The recipe originally used at Manca's remains a family secret, but now people call all types of oven pancakes "Dutch babies"—no matter what size they are.

The batter we use here is full of eggs and puffs up dramatically in the oven. The results are even more spectacular when the batter is baked in a big container such as a paella pan. If you don't have a paella pan, you can use a big iron frying pan, a large baking dish, or even a foil roasting pan. Any shape will do, but the container must be fairly shallow—not much more than 3 inches deep.

Once you decide on a pan, measure its total volume by pouring in quarts of water. When you've determined the pan's volume, select the recipe proportions you need from the chart below. Then get out the ingredients and you're ready to start.

Pan Size	Butter	Eggs	Milk & Flour
2-3 qt.	¼ cup	3	¾ cup *each*
3-4 qt.	⅓ cup	4	1 cup *each*
4-4½ qt.	½ cup	5	1¼ cups *each*
4½-5 qt.	½ cup	6	1½ cups *each*

This pancake is so spectacular when it first comes out of the oven, you'll want to have everyone seated before you bring it to the table. You can serve it with fruit topping, either spooned over or served alongside, and you can round out your menu with browned sausages, crisp bacon strips, or pan-fried ham slices.

To make, place butter in pan and set in a 425° oven. While butter melts, mix batter quickly. Put eggs in a blender or food processor and whirl at high speed for 1 minute. With motor running, gradually pour in milk, then slowly add flour; continue whirling for 30 seconds. Or, in a bowl, beat eggs until blended; gradually beat in milk, then flour.

Remove pan from oven and pour in batter. Return pan to oven and bake until pancake is puffy and well browned (20 to 25 minutes, depending on pan size).

Dust pancake with ground nutmeg, if you wish. Cut in wedges and serve at once with any of the following toppings. Makes 3 to 6 servings.

Powdered sugar classic. Have a shaker or bowl of **powdered sugar** and thick wedges of **lemon** at the table. Sprinkle sugar on hot pancake, then squeeze on lemon juice.

Fruit. Sliced strawberries or peaches, sweetened to taste; or any fruits in season, cut and sweetened. Or substitute canned or frozen fruit.

Hot fruit. Glazed apples or pears (page 4) make a good topping; offer with **sour cream** or yogurt. Or heat **banana** or **papaya** slices in melted **butter** or margarine over medium heat, turning until hot; serve with **lime** wedges.

Canned pie filling. To **cherry or apple pie filling,** add **lemon juice** and **ground cinnamon** to taste. Serve cold or warm, topped with **yogurt** or sour cream.

Syrups. Pass warm or cold **honey,** maple syrup, or any favorite fruit sauce (pages 52-53).

Basic Crêpes *(French Pancakes)*

Though crêpe-making is time consuming, you can make crêpes days—even months—ahead and freeze them until you are ready to use them. Then let the package of crêpes come to room temperature before you separate them into individual pancakes so they won't stick and tear.

> 1 **cup milk**
> 3 **eggs**
> ⅔ **cup all-purpose flour**
> **About 4 teaspoons butter or margarine**

In blender, whirl milk, eggs, and flour until smooth. (Or blend eggs and milk with a wire whip; add flour and mix until smooth.) Let rest, at room temperature, for at least 1 hour. (Or cover and refrigerate until next day; bring batter to room temperature before cooking.)

Place a 6 or 7-inch crêpe pan or other flat-bottomed frying pan on medium heat. When hot, add ¼ teaspoon butter and swirl to coat surface. Stir batter and pour in about 2 tablespoons, quickly tilting pan so batter flows over entire flat surface. If heat is correct and pan hot enough, crêpe sets at once, forming tiny bubbles (don't worry if there are a few little holes); if pan is too cold, batter makes a smooth layer. Cook until surface is dry and edge is lightly browned. Turn with a spatula and brown other side. Turn out onto a plate, stacking crêpes as made. If made ahead, cool, then place wax paper between each crêpe; package airtight (in quantities you expect to use) and refriger-ate for as long as a week; or freeze for longer storage. Allow crêpes to come to room temperature before separating; they tear if cold.

To serve, spread with butter and jam or enclose with a filling (below., and pages 47-48) for a main dish entrée. Makes 12 to 16 crêpes.

Crab-filled Crêpes

Nothing masks the distinctive crab flavor in these quick and simple filled crêpes. Buttery avocado slices and cold sour cream accent each one.

> 1 **dozen crêpes (see preceding recipe)**
> 1 **pound cooked crab meat**
> 1¼ **cups sour cream**
> 6 **tablespoons freshly grated Parmesan cheese**
> 2 **firm-ripe avocados**
> 2 **tablespoons lemon juice**

Make crêpes. Combine crab with ¾ cup of the sour cream. Spoon 2 rounded tablespoons of crab mixture across lower third of each crêpe and roll to enclose (see Folding Method 2 below). Place filled crêpes, seam side down, in a lightly greased 9 by 13-inch baking pan. Evenly sprinkle with cheese. Cover and bake in a 400° oven for 20 minutes.

While crêpes are baking, peel, pit, and slice avocados; coat slices with lemon juice. To serve, spoon some of the remaining ½ cup sour cream over each crêpe and top with several slices of avocado. Makes 1 dozen crêpes.

How to fold crepes

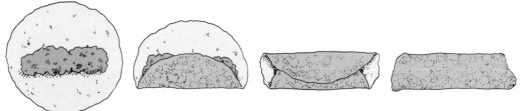

METHOD 1. Mound filling across center of crêpe. Fold one side over filling, then fold opposite side over. Place seam side down in baking dish.

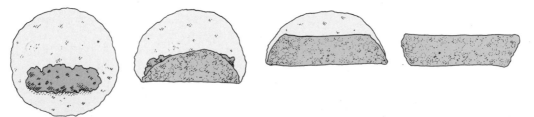

METHOD 2. Mound filling across lower third of crêpe. Fold lower edge over filling, then roll to enclose. Place seam side down in baking dish.

Fruity Cheese-filled Crêpes

Apples, oranges, and raisins are enhanced with spices and cooked until tender in this make-ahead crêpe filling. Sliced almonds give the mixture a crunchy texture. Both parts of this filling are made a day in advance, so flavors blend and raisins plump to fullness. The following day, assemble crêpes, cook briefly, and serve. Top with orange marmalade and a dollop of sour cream, if desired.

    10 basic crêpes (page 45)
     4 ounces cream cheese, softened
    ½ cup sour cream
     3 tablespoons powdered sugar
     5 medium-size (about 1¾ lbs. total) golden delicious
        apples
    ¼ cup orange juice
     1 small orange, peeled, cut into ⅛-inch rounds, and
        seeded
    ½ cup raisins
    ⅓ cup slivered almonds
     1 teaspoon ground cinnamon
    ½ teaspoon ground nutmeg
     3 tablespoons granulated sugar
        Orange marmalade (optional)
        Sour cream (optional)

Make crêpes. In a small bowl, beat cream cheese, sour cream, and powdered sugar until smooth. Cover and refrigerate until next day.

Peel, core, and shred apples (a food processor does the job quickly). Place shredded apples in a 2½-quart pan along with orange juice, orange rounds, raisins, almonds, cinnamon, nutmeg, and granulated sugar; blend well. Bring to a boil over medium-high heat. Cover pan and reduce heat to medium; cook for about 15 minutes or until apples are fork tender. Uncover pan and cook, stirring constantly, until most of the liquid has evaporated. Cool, cover, and refrigerate until next day.

To assemble, spoon 2 rounded tablespoons of fruit filling down center of each crêpe. Top fruit with 1 rounded tablespoon of the cheese mixture. Fold in each crêpe edge toward center (see Folding Method 1 page 45). Place crêpes seam side down in a lightly greased 9 by 13-inch baking pan. Cover and bake in a 350° oven for about 30 minutes or until heated through. Serve with orange marmalade and sour cream, if desired. Makes 10 crêpes.

DUTCH BABY PUFFS UP dramatically in the oven, evolving into a golden-crusted, moist-centered superpancake. Fresh fruit is splendid as a topping, or it can be served alongside. To complete the menu, browned sausages and orange juice. The Dutch Baby recipe is on page 44.

Golden Apple-filled Crêpes

Golden delicious apples, accented with lemon and nutmeg, are cooked just until tender, then used as a filling for crêpes.

        About 8 basic crêpes (page 45)
     5 medium-size golden delicious apples
     2 tablespoons butter or margarine
     1 teaspoon grated lemon peel
     1 tablespoon lemon juice
    ⅛ teaspoon ground nutmeg
    ½ cup sugar
     2 tablespoons brandy (optional)

Make crêpes. Peel, core, and cut apples into ½-inch-thick slices; you should have 6 cups. In a large frying pan over medium heat, melt butter. Add apple slices, lemon peel, lemon juice, and nutmeg. Cook, gently turning occasionally with a wide spatula, until apples begin to soften and look translucent (about 7 minutes). Add sugar and cook, stirring gently, for 2 more minutes.

Warm brandy, if used; then ignite and spoon flaming liquid over apples. Continue cooking until liquid is reduced to about 2 tablespoons; cool. If made ahead, cover and refrigerate for as long as 2 days.

To assemble, have apple filling and crêpes at room temperature. Spoon 3 tablespoons of filling across lower third of each crêpe and roll to enclose (see Folding Method 2 page 45). Place filled crêpes, seam side down, in a lightly buttered baking dish. Spoon remaining filling over top, cover and bake in a 325° oven for 25 minutes or until crêpes are heated through. Makes 8 crêpes.

Cheese Blintzes with Cherry Sauce

Golden on the outside, creamy on the inside—that's the best way to characterize these intriguing Russian-Jewish blintzes. The cheese filling is flavored by onions cooked mellow, sweet, and amber; the topping is hot cherry sauce and cold sour cream. You can shape the blintzes a day ahead, but they should be cooked just before serving.

        Cheese filling (directions follow)
    20 to 24 basic crêpes (page 45 ; but use 1½ times the
        recipe and *cook each crêpe on one side only,* until
        dry on top side)
        Sweet cherry sauce (directions follow)
        About 6 tablespoons *each* salad oil and butter or
        margarine
        Sour cream

(Continued on page 49)

Filled crêpes from the freezer: Bake without thawing

It's reassuring to have completely prepared entrées in the freezer, dishes that can be ready to serve in a very short time. That's the advantage of these filled crêpes. You freeze them individually, then bake (without thawing) as many as you need.

To freeze, place the crêpes, seam side down and slightly apart, on a greased baking sheet and freeze until firm. Then package airtight and return to freezer; use within 2 weeks.

Mushroom Crêpes

These savory mushroom crêpes make a delightful entrée served with a side dish of ham or sausage, or topped with a poached egg.

- 12 to 16 basic crêpes (page 45)
- 3 pounds mushrooms
- 4 tablespoons butter or margarine
- 1 large onion, chopped
- 2 cloves garlic, minced or pressed
- ¾ teaspoon marjoram leaves
- ¼ cup all-purpose flour
- ¾ cup milk
- 3 tablespoons dry sherry
- ½ cup grated Parmesan cheese
- ¼ cup chopped parsley
  Salt and pepper to taste
- 1 cup (4 oz.) shredded Swiss cheese

Prepare crêpes (or bring to room temperature, if refrigerated). Chop mushroom stems, slice caps, and reserve in separate pile. In a wide frying pan over medium heat, melt 2 tablespoons of the butter. Add mushroom stems, onion, and garlic; cook, stirring, until onion is limp. Add remaining 2 tablespoons butter, sliced mushroom caps, and marjoram; cook, stirring, until mushrooms are limp. Sprinkle flour over mushrooms and cook, stirring, until bubbly. Gradually stir in milk; then cook, stirring, until sauce boils and thickens. Remove from heat. Add sherry, Parmesan cheese, and parsley. Cool; then season to taste with salt and pepper.

Evenly divide filling among crêpes, spooning it down the center of each; fold to enclose (see Method 1, page 45). If made ahead, freeze according to preceding directions.

To bake, arrange desired number of fresh or frozen crêpes in a lightly greased shallow casserole dish or in individual ramekins. Cover and bake in a 375° oven for 15 to 20 minutes (25 to 30 minutes, if frozen). Remove cover, sprinkle each crêpe with about 1 tablespoon Swiss cheese, and bake for 5 minutes longer or until cheese melts. Makes 6 to 8 servings of 2 crêpes each.

Chicken Crêpes

Tender crêpes enclose a hearty filling of chicken and vegetables.

- 12 to 16 basic crêpes (page 45)
- 5 tablespoons butter or margarine
- 1 small onion, chopped
- ¼ pound mushrooms, sliced
- 3 tablespoons all-purpose flour
- ⅔ cup chicken broth
- ½ cup half-and-half (light cream)
- 1 package (8 oz.) frozen artichoke hearts, thawed and drained
- 2 cups diced, cooked chicken or turkey
- ⅓ cup grated Parmesan cheese
- ¼ teaspoon dry rosemary
- ½ teaspoon salt
- ½ cup shredded Swiss cheese

Prepare crêpes (or bring to room temperature, if refrigerated). In a wide frying pan over medium heat, melt 2 tablespoons of the butter. Add onion and mushrooms. Cook, stirring, until mushrooms are limp. Stir in the remaining 3 tablespoons of butter until melted. Add flour; cook, stirring, until bubbly. Gradually stir in broth and half-and-half; cook, stirring, until it boils and thickens, then remove from heat. Cut artichokes into thirds; add to sauce along with chicken, Parmesan cheese, rosemary, and salt; cool.

Evenly divide filling among crêpes, spooning it down the center of each; fold to enclose (see Method 1, page 45). If made ahead, freeze according to preceding directions.

To bake, arrange desired number of fresh or frozen crêpes in a lightly greased shallow casserole dish or individual ramekins. Cover and bake in a 375° oven for about 20 minutes (35 to 40 minutes, if frozen). Remove cover, evenly distribute about 1 tablespoon Swiss cheese over top of each crêpe. Return to oven just until cheese melts. Makes 6 to 8 servings of 2 crêpes each.

Prepare cheese filling, make crêpes, then prepare sweet cherry sauce. Spoon 3 tablespoons of cheese filling in a rectangular mound in center of browned side of each crêpe. Enclose filling by folding opposite sides of crêpe up and over the filling to make a rectangular bundle (see illustrations below).

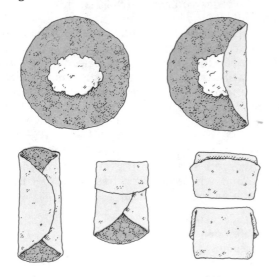

In a wide frying pan over high heat, melt 3 tablespoons of the butter in about 3 tablespoons of the oil. Place blintzes, seam side down, in pan (without crowding). Fry until golden brown on each side (about 2 minutes total). Transfer to a platter and keep warm until all are cooked. Add more butter and oil to pan as needed.

Spoon sour cream onto each serving of blintzes and top with hot sweet cherry sauce. Makes 20 to 24 blintzes (6 or 7 servings).

Cheese filling. Finely chop 1 large **onion.** In a frying pan over medium heat, melt 2 tablespoons **butter** or margarine. Add onion and cook, stirring frequently, for about 20 minutes or until golden brown. Transfer cooked onions and butter to a large bowl, add 1 large package (8 oz.) **cream cheese** and 1½ pounds **pot cheese** (also called farmer's cheese), and beat until smoothly blended. Makes about 4 cups filling.

Instead of pot cheese, you can use 2 pints (4 cups) large curd cottage cheese, dried as follows: spread cheese on a muslin cloth (such as a tea towel); wrap up in cloth and twist to wring out as much moisture from cheese as possible; unwrap and scrape cheese from cloth.

Sweet cherry sauce. Pit 2 to 3 cups **bing cherries,** or drain 1 can (1 lb.) pitted sweet cherries. In a pan, combine 2 teaspoons **cornstarch,** ¼ cup **sugar,** ½ cup **water** (if using canned cherries, use ½ cup of the syrup instead of sugar and water), and 2 teaspoons **lemon juice.** Place pan over very high heat and bring to a rapid boil, stirring, until sauce is thickened. Use hot, or set aside and reheat to simmering.

Basic Pancakes & Waffles

(Pictured on page 3)

Easy to make with ingredients you have on hand, this basic recipe can be used for pancakes or waffles. Variations on the basic recipe follow. Choose from the variety of homemade toppers provided on pages 52-53.

- 1⅓ **cups all-purpose flour**
- 2 **teaspoons baking powder**
- ½ **teaspoon salt**
- 1 **tablespoon sugar**
- 2 **eggs, separated**
- 1 **to 1¼ cups milk**
- 3 **tablespoons salad oil**

In a medium-size bowl, combine flour, baking powder, salt, and sugar; set aside.

In a medium-size bowl, beat egg whites just until stiff, moist peaks form. In another bowl, without washing beaters, beat yolks lightly. Stir in milk (use 1 cup for waffles, 1¼ cups for pancakes) and oil; blend well. Add liquid mixture to dry ingredients; beat until smooth. Fold in beaten whites.

For pancakes, preheat a griddle or large frying pan over medium heat; grease lightly. Spoon batter, about 3 tablespoons for each cake, onto griddle; spread batter to make 4-inch circles. Cook until tops are bubbly and appear dry; turn and cook other sides until browned. Makes about 1 dozen pancakes.

For waffles, bake in a preheated waffle iron according to manufacturer's directions. Makes about 10 4-inch-square waffles.

Blueberry. Stir ½ to ¾ cup fresh or well-drained canned or frozen **blueberries** into batter. Bake as directed for pancakes or waffles.

Bacon. Cook 6 to 8 strips **bacon;** drain on paper towels, then crumble and stir into batter. Bake as directed for pancakes or waffles.

Cheese. Make basic recipe but omit sugar and add 1 cup (4 oz.) shredded **Cheddar cheese.** Bake as directed for pancakes or waffles.

Blueberry-topped Orange Waffles

For a light meal, serve these crisp and tender orange-flavored waffles topped with sweetened whipped cream and fresh or frozen blueberries. Accompany with browned sausage links or crisp bacon strips, if you wish.

(Continued on next page)

2 cups all-purpose flour
¼ cup sugar
1 teaspoon *each* baking powder and soda
½ teaspoon salt
4 eggs
1 tablespoon grated orange peel
1¼ cups orange juice
2 tablespoons lemon juice
¼ cup butter or margarine, melted and cooled
   Whipped cream topping (directions follow)
2 to 3 cups fresh or frozen blueberries

In a medium-size bowl, stir together flour, sugar, baking powder, soda, and salt; set aside. In a large bowl, beat eggs; stir in orange peel, orange juice, and lemon juice. Add egg mixture to flour mixture; beat until well blended. Stir in butter.

Bake waffles in a preheated waffle iron according to manufacturer's directions. Serve hot. Pass whipped cream topping and blueberries to spoon over top. Makes about 14 4-inch-square waffles.

Whipped cream topping. In a bowl, whip ½ pint **whipping cream.** Gently fold in until blended: 3 tablespoons sifted **powdered sugar** and 2 teaspoons *each* **grated orange peel** and **grated lemon peel.**

Bran-Wheat Waffles

Whole wheat flour and bran give these waffles a sweet nutty flavor and a crunchy texture. They can be baked ahead and frozen for later use. Simply reheat and recrisp the frozen waffles in a toaster. Spread with butter and top with syrup or preserves to eat like toast.

⅔ cup *each* all-purpose flour and whole wheat flour
¾ cup unprocessed bran
1 tablespoon baking powder
½ teaspoon salt
2 eggs, separated
¼ cup firmly packed brown sugar
1½ cups milk
⅓ cup butter or margarine, melted and cooled.

In a large bowl, stir together all-purpose flour and whole wheat flour, bran, baking powder, and salt. In a medium-size bowl, lightly beat egg yolks and sugar; stir in milk and butter. Stir yolk mixture into flour mixture just until moistened; do not beat.

In a small bowl, beat egg whites just until stiff, moist peaks form; fold gently into batter. Bake waffles in a preheated waffle iron according to manufacturer's directions. Serve hot.

Or cool on wire racks, package airtight, and freeze. To serve, heat waffles (unthawed) in toaster until crisp and hot. Makes about 8 4-inch square waffles.

Belgian Waffles

(Pictured on opposite page)

Delicious attractions in Belgium are the deeply indented waffles you can purchase at sidewalk stands and carnival food booths. You can bake these waffles in a standard electric waffle iron, but if you want authentic, thick Belgian waffles with their characteristic deep indentations, you'll need a special Belgian waffle iron, available in gourmet cookware shops and in some department store housewares sections. You place this iron over direct heat to bake the waffles atop the range. Our version of Belgian waffles is light and moist—best described as a cross between a popover and a batter cake. Add a sprinkle of powdered sugar, lightly sweetened whipped cream, and whole or sliced fresh strawberries and you have an irresistible treat.

4 eggs, separated
2 tablespoons granulated sugar
½ teaspoon salt
1 cup milk
½ teaspoon vanilla or almond extract
4 tablespoons butter or margarine, melted and cooled
1 cup all-purpose flour
   Melted butter or margarine
   Powdered sugar
   Sweetened whipped cream (optional)
   Strawberries, whole or sliced (optional)

In a medium-size bowl, beat egg whites just until stiff, moist peaks form; set aside.

In a large bowl, combine egg yolks, granulated sugar, and salt. Beat yolk mixture until thick; blend in milk, vanilla, and the 4 tablespoons butter. Continue beating while gradually adding flour; blend well. Gently fold in beaten egg whites.

Place a seasoned (page 57) Belgian waffle iron directly over medium-high heat, turning it over occasionally until water dripped inside sizzles (or preheat a standard waffle iron according to manufacturer's directions). Open iron and brush grids lightly with melted butter. Spoon ⅔ cup batter into Belgian iron (or recommended amount of batter into electric iron), spreading batter just to cover grids. Close and turn Belgian waffle iron over every 30 seconds until waffle is richly browned (about 3 to 4 minutes); open iron during last 2 minutes to check for doneness. (Or bake according to manufacturer's directions for an electric waffle iron.) Let cool slightly and dust with powdered sugar; top with whipped cream and strawberries, if you wish. Makes 5 Belgian waffles, about 4 by 6 inches.

THE SIMPLEST, FRESHEST ADORNMENTS —strawberries and whipped cream—accompany traditional Belgian Waffles. For a wintertime variation, substitute frozen or canned fruit for fresh berries. The recipe is above.

Homemade toppers

(Pictured on page 54)

Flavored butters, syrups, sauces, and cream toppings ...these homemade specialties give your menu new and exciting flavors, and they'll make your griddle cakes, toasts, rolls, and breads even more delicious. All of them can be made in a few minutes. Some are refrigerated overnight to blend flavors, then served cold; others are simmered for a few minutes and served hot.

Flavored Butters

Here are six cool, fluffy butter spreads to top off your hot griddle cakes, toasts, rolls, and breads. Each spread starts out with ½ cup of softened butter or margarine that is then laced with spices, fruits, or nuts. Naturally, flavored butters spread more easily and melt faster when they are at room temperature.

Cinnamon butter. Beat ½ cup softened **butter** or margarine with 1 teaspoon **ground cinnamon** and 3 tablespoons **powdered sugar** until fluffy.

Date-nut butter. In a small bowl, beat together until fluffy ½ cup softened **butter** or margarine; 3 tablespoons *each* **powdered sugar** and finely chopped **pitted dates;** and ¼ cup finely chopped **pecans** or walnuts.

Honey butter. In a small bowl, beat ½ cup softened **butter** or margarine with ¼ cup **honey** until fluffy.

Orange butter. In a small bowl, beat ½ cup softened **butter** or margarine with 1½ teaspoons **grated orange peel** and 3 tablespoons **powdered sugar** until fluffy.

Peach or nectarine butter. Peel, pit, and chop 1 medium-size **peach** or nectarine; you should have ½ cup. Place fruit in blender container or food processor. Add 1 teaspoon **lemon juice,** ½ cup **butter** or margarine cut into chunks, 2 tablespoons firmly packed **brown sugar** or honey, and ¼ teaspoon **ground nutmeg;** blend until fluffy. (Butter will not be perfectly smooth.) Cover and chill for as long as 6 hours to blend flavors.

Spicy butter. In a small bowl, beat until fluffy ½ cup softened **butter** or margarine; 3 tablespoons firmly packed **brown** sugar; ¼ teaspoon *each* **ground cinnamon** and **allspice;** and ⅛ teaspoon **ground nutmeg.**

Syrups

What icing is to a cake, syrup is to pancakes, waffles, or French toast. Add a touch of sweetness to your hotcakes with these four quick and easy syrups. Our maple-flavored syrup is thinner than the commercially prepared syrup, and you can adjust the maple flavoring to suit your own taste. It thickens upon cooling and should be kept refrigerated. The lemon-honey syrup is a sweet topping that goes well over the basic pancakes and waffles (page 49) or the cornmeal waffles (page 55). Serve these lemon-honey/ginger-orange syrups warm, but keep them stored in the refrigerator and reheat just before serving.

Apple cider syrup. In a small pan, combine ¾ cup **apple cider;** ½ cup *each* firmly packed **brown sugar** and light **corn syrup;** 2 tablespoons **butter** or margarine; ½ teaspoon **lemon juice;** and ⅛ teaspoon *each* **ground cinnamon** and **ground nutmeg.** Bring mixture to a boil, uncovered, over medium-high heat. Reduce heat and simmer, uncovered, for 15 minutes or until thickened. Serve warm. Makes about 1½ cups.

Lemon-honey syrup. In a small pan, combine 1 cup **honey,** 6 tablespoons **butter** or margarine, and 4 teaspoons **lemon juice;** cook uncovered, over medium-high heat, stirring frequently, until butter melts and syrup is smooth. Makes about 1½ cups.

Orange-honey syrup. In a small pan, combine 1 cup **honey,** ⅓ cup **orange juice,** 1 tablespoon **butter** or margarine, and ¼ teaspoon **grated orange peel.** Cook, uncovered over medium-high heat, stirring frequently, until butter melts and syrup is smooth. Makes about 1½ cups.

Maple-flavored syrup. In a small pan, combine 2 cups **sugar,** 1 cup **water,** and 3 tablespoons **light corn syrup.** Bring to a boil, uncovered, over medium-high heat; boil for 3 minutes. Remove from heat and stir in ½ to ¾ teaspoon **imitation maple flavoring.** It thickens upon cooling. Makes about 1½ cups.

Ginger-orange syrup. Peel and shred enough **fresh ginger** to make about 2 tablespoons. In a small pan, combine ginger, ½ teaspoon **grated orange peel,** ½ cup *each* **orange juice** and **water,** 2 tablespoons **light**

corn syrup, and 1 cup sugar. Bring to a boil, uncovered, over medium-high heat; boil for 5 minutes. Makes about 1½ cups.

Sauces

Instead of standing over a hot range for hours cooking fresh fruit jams, try these simple and quick ideas for fruit sauces.

The raspberry sauce and strawberry sauce are made in minutes with frozen presweetened berries that have been thawed. "Mildly sweet" best describes the strawberry sauce, and the raspberry sauce has a slight tartness. Both of these sauces thicken upon cooling and are best served cold.

The hot tangy pineapple sauce and the buttery pear sauce are made from canned fruit. Keep your pantry shelf stocked with cans of pears and crushed pineapple for a sauce you can have table-ready in just 10 minutes. Like the lemon filling in a lemon meringue pie, the taste of the hot lemon sauce is sweet and sour.

Raspberry or strawberry sauce. In a small pan, combine 1 package (about 10 oz.) frozen presweetened **raspberries** or strawberries, thawed; ½ teaspoon **cornstarch;** and 1 tablespoon **light corn syrup.** Bring to a rolling boil over medium-high heat; boil, stirring constantly, for 2 minutes. Remove from heat; then cool, cover, and refrigerate. This sauce thickens as it cools. Serve cold. Makes about 1 cup.

Blueberry sauce. In a pan, combine ⅓ cup **sugar** and 1 tablespoon **cornstarch;** add 2 cups fresh or frozen and thawed **blueberries,** 2 tablespoons **lemon juice,** and ⅓ cup **water.** Cook over medium heat, stirring, until mixture is thickened. Serve warm or cold. Makes about 2 cups sauce.

Lemon sauce. In a small pan, combine ⅓ cup **sugar** and 1 tablespoon **cornstarch;** stir in 1 cup **boiling water** and 2 teaspoons **grated lemon peel.** Cook over medium heat, stirring, until slightly thickened and clear. Remove from heat; stir in 1 tablespoon **butter** or margarine and 2 tablespoons **lemon juice.** Serve warm. Makes about 1 cup.

Pear sauce. In a small pan over medium heat, melt 4 tablespoons **butter** or margarine. Add 3 tablespoons firmly packed **brown sugar;** stir until sugar dissolves. Drain 1 can (13 oz.) **pear halves,** reserving ⅓ cup of the syrup; set pears aside. In a small bowl, blend reserved syrup with ½ teaspoon *each* **ground cinnamon** and **cornstarch;** add to butter mixture and stir to blend. Chop pears; add to sauce in pan. Cook, stirring, for about 5 minutes or until mixture is thickened. Serve warm. Makes about 1¼ cups.

Pineapple sauce. In a small pan over medium heat, melt 3 tablespoons **butter** or margarine. Add 2 tablespoons firmly packed **brown sugar;** stir until sugar dissolves. Add 1 can (about 8 oz.) **crushed pineapple** and the syrup, and ⅛ teaspoon ground **nutmeg.** Cook for 5 minutes or until some of the liquid has evaporated. Serve warm. Makes about 1 cup.

Cream & Fruit Toppings

Here is something special to crown your pancakes, waffles, or French toast: cool, sweetened cream toppings over fruit. The lime topping is a refreshing, flavored whipped cream which goes over fresh fruit slices of the season. A stiffly beaten egg white keeps the topping fluffy. For a tangy flavor, try orange and sour cream topping over juicy sliced strawberries. Serve over sourdough waffles (page 56), or Belgian waffles (page 50).

Lime topping. In a medium bowl, beat 1 cup **whipping cream** just until soft peaks form. Beat in 3 tablespoons **powdered sugar** and 2 teaspoons **grated lime peel** just until blended. Cover and chill.

To serve, beat 1 **egg white** just until stiff, moist peaks form; gently fold into cream mixture. Pour into a serving bowl to accompany fresh fruit. At the table, we suggest passing a bowl of mixed fresh fruit, such as strawberry halves, slices of papaya, and pineapple chunks — or other fruit that is in season. Let guests embellish their pancakes or waffles with fruit, and then pass the bowl of fluffy lime topping to crown each entrée. Makes 2½ cups topping.

Orange and sour cream topping. In a small bowl, combine 1 cup **sour cream,** 3 teaspoons **frozen orange juice concentrate,** and 1 tablespoon **powdered sugar;** blend well, cover, and chill for at least 4 hours to blend flavors.

To serve, we suggest passing a bowl of fresh strawberries with the orange and sour cream topping; then let guests embellish their pancakes or waffles with fruit, then add topping to crown each entrée. Makes about 1 cup topping.

Cornmeal Waffles

Wheat germ and cornmeal give these whole grain waffles a crunchy texture. Top waffles with lemon-honey syrup (page 52) and fresh fruit slices, if desired, and serve ham slices alongside.

    2 eggs, separated
    2 cups buttermilk
    1 cup whole wheat or unbleached white flour
    ¾ cup cornmeal
    2 teaspoons baking powder
    1 teaspoon soda
    ½ teaspoon salt
    2 tablespoons sugar
    ¼ cup wheat germ
    6 tablespoons butter or margarine, melted and cooled

In a medium-size bowl, beat egg yolks and buttermilk until blended. In another medium-size bowl, stir together flour, cornmeal, baking powder, soda, salt, sugar, and wheat germ. Gradually add flour mixture to yolk mixture; blending until smooth. Stir in butter.

In a small bowl, beat egg whites just until stiff, moist peaks form; fold into cornmeal batter just until blended. Bake waffles in a preheated waffle iron according to manufacturer's directions. Serve hot. Makes about 1 dozen 4-inch-square waffles.

Gingerbread Waffles

Spicy gingerbread waffles are topped with a ginger cream that can be made a day in advance. Accompany with sweetened applesauce and crisp bacon strips.

    ¼ cup butter or margarine
    ½ cup *each* firmly packed dark brown sugar and light molasses
    2 eggs, separated
    1 cup milk
    2 cups all-purpose flour
    1½ teaspoons baking powder
    1 teaspoon *each* ground cinnamon and ground ginger
    ¼ teaspoon *each* ground cloves and salt
       Ginger cream (directions follow)

In a large bowl, beat together butter and brown sugar. Beat in molasses, egg yolks, and milk. Sift

flour with baking powder, cinnamon, ginger, cloves and salt.

In a medium-size bowl, beat egg whites with clean beaters until stiff, moist peaks form. Stir flour mixture into yolk mixture; fold in beaten whites. Bake waffles in a preheated waffle iron according to manufacturer's directions. Makes 8 4-inch-square waffles.

Ginger cream. Whip 1 cup **whipping cream** with 2 teaspoons **sugar.** Fold in 2 tablespoons finely chopped **crystallized ginger.** Place in a serving bowl to pass at the table. This can be made a day in advance and refrigerated until ready to serve.

Scandinavian Heart-shaped Waffles

A special waffle iron is responsible for the unique appearance of these crisp heart-shaped waffles. You can purchase the iron in gourmet cookware shops or department store housewares sections. But you can certainly use this batter in a standard electric waffle iron, too.

The cream-based waffle literally explodes in the iron, then holds its fragile form with the aid of baking powder. These waffles can be made ahead and served warm or cold. Traditionally they are topped with whipped cream and berries.

    1¼ cups all-purpose flour
    ¾ cup water
    1¼ cups whipping cream
    2 tablespoons sugar
    1½ teaspoons vanilla
    2¼ teaspoons baking powder
       Dash of salt

In a large bowl, beat together flour and water until smooth. Stir in ¼ cup of the whipping cream, along with sugar, vanilla, baking powder, and salt. In a medium bowl, beat the remaining 1 cup whipping cream until stiff; then fold into batter and let stand for 10 minutes.

Place a seasoned (page 57) heart-shaped waffle iron over medium-high heat, turning it over until water sprinkled inside sizzles (or preheat an electric waffle iron according to manufacturer's directions).

Open heart iron and spoon in about ⅓ cup batter (or use amount recommended for other shaped grids and bake according to manufacturer's directions). Close heart iron, squeezing handles gently, then turn iron over about every 30 seconds until waffle is golden brown (about 4 minutes). After first 4 turns, open iron often to check for doneness. Transfer waffles to a wire rack. Serve warm or cooled. Makes 8 to 10 whole heart-shaped waffles.

SWEET AND LUSCIOUS, these toppers include (clockwise from bottom left) Strawberry Sauce, honey, Blueberry Sauce, Orange Honey Syrup, Ginger Orange Syrup, Raspberry Sauce, Apple Cider Syrup, and Maple-flavored Syrup. Bees made the honey; you can make all the other toppers using the recipes on pages 52-53.

Granola Waffles

The delightful nutty flavor of these nutritious waffles comes from the combination of granola cereal and whole wheat. The batter is thicker than most and makes a heartier, chewier waffle. Serve piping hot with orange-honey syrup (page 52).

- ¾ cup granola (page 85 or purchased)
- 1 cup whole wheat flour
- 1¾ cups all-purpose flour
- 1 teaspoon *each* salt and grated orange peel
- 2 teaspoons baking powder
- 2 eggs
- 2 cups milk
- ½ cup butter or margarine, melted and cooled
- 2 tablespoons honey

In a medium-size bowl, combine granola, whole wheat flour, all-purpose flour, salt, orange peel, and baking powder; set aside.

Break eggs into a large bowl; beat eggs lightly with a rotary or electric mixer. Beat in milk, butter, and honey until blended. Add the flour mixture and beat until batter is smooth. Bake waffles in a preheated waffle iron according to manufacturer's directions. Makes 9 or 10 4-inch-square waffles.

Sourdough Waffles

These sourdough waffles are so light and crisp they simply shatter when you bite into them. You start the batter the night before with sourdough starter (page 68), flour, and water. If you have any leftover waffles, store them in an airtight package in the freezer; then reheat in a toaster until recrisped. Top them with a flavored butter, syrup, or fruit preserves (pages 52–53). Crisp bacon strips and chilled tomato juice make good accompaniments.

- ¾ cup sourdough starter (page 68)
- 1½ cups warm water (about 110°)
- 1¾ cups all-purpose flour
- 2 eggs
- ¼ cup salad oil or melted butter or margarine (cooled)
- ¾ teaspoon *each* salt and soda
- 1½ tablespoons sugar

In a 3-quart bowl, combine sourdough starter, water, and flour; cover and set in a warm place (about 85°), such as inside the oven with the light turned on, and leave overnight.

Just before baking, carefully separate eggs. Stir egg yolks and oil into sourdough mixture. In a small cup, combine salt, soda, and sugar; set aside. In a medium-size bowl, beat egg whites just until stiff, moist peaks form.

Stir soda mixture into batter, then gently fold in beaten whites. Bake waffles in a preheated waffle iron according to manufacturer's directions. Makes 8 4-inch-square waffles.

Crisp Banana Waffles

Bananas are on the inside and spooned atop these hot and crispy waffles. You can embellish them at the table with butter and maple syrup, and accompany with browned sausages.

- 1 cup all-purpose flour
- 2 teaspoons baking powder
- ½ teaspoon salt
- ¼ teaspoon *each* ground cinnamon and ground nutmeg
- 2 tablespoons sugar
- 2 eggs, separated
- 1 cup milk
- 1 cup mashed banana (about 2 large bananas)
- 6 tablespoons butter or margarine, melted and cooled
  About 6 bananas
  Lemon juice
- 1 cup chopped almonds or macadamia nuts

In a small bowl, stir together flour, baking powder, salt, cinnamon, nutmeg, and sugar; set aside. In a medium-size bowl, beat egg yolks and milk until blended. Add flour mixture and stir until blended. Stir in mashed bananas and butter. In a third bowl, beat egg whites with clean beaters until just stiff, moist peaks form; fold into batter. Bake waffles in a preheated waffle iron according to manufacturer's directions.

While waffles bake, prepare bananas. Peel bananas and cut into ¼-inch slices; place in serving bowl. Sprinkle lemon juice over bananas (to prevent browning) and toss lightly to coat. Put nuts in another serving bowl to pass at the table. Makes 1 dozen 4-inch-square waffles.

Eggnog Waffles

These flavorful and tender eggnog waffles are quick to prepare and delicious to eat. You make them with commercial eggnog. Purchase refrigerated eggnog when it's available and freeze for as long as 2 months in the original carton; then thaw in refrigerator and stir before using. Or use the canned eggnog that's available in some markets all year.

  2 **cups baking mix (biscuit mix)**
 ¼ **teaspoon ground nutmeg**
  2 **tablespoons salad oil**
1½ **cups commercial eggnog**
  1 **egg**

In a bowl, combine baking mix, nutmeg, salad oil, eggnog, and egg; beat until smooth. Bake waffles in a preheated waffle iron according to manufacturer's directions. Makes 8 4-inch-square waffles.

Sour Cream Waffles with Shrimp-Mushroom Topping

Tender sour cream waffles serve as a base for a rich and creamy shrimp-mushroom topping. Have all the ingredients for the topping ready to go before starting to cook, then make the topping while you bake the waffles. These waffles are also good plain, with melted butter and syrup. Consider serving them with chilled melon wedges and orange sections to complete the menu.

1½ **cups all-purpose flour**
  1 **teaspoon baking powder**
 ¾ **teaspoon** *each* **soda and salt**
 ½ **teaspoon caraway seed**
  2 **eggs, lightly beaten**
  1 **cup sour cream**
 ½ **cup milk**
 ¼ **cup salad oil**
    Shrimp-mushroom topping (directions follow)

In a large bowl, mix flour with baking powder, soda, and salt. Add caraway seed. In a medium-size bowl, mix eggs, sour cream, milk, and oil; blend well and pour all at once into flour mixture. Stir batter until smooth.

Bake in a preheated waffle iron according to manufacturer's directions. Keep waffles warm in a 200°

oven until all are baked. While waffles are baking, make shrimp-mushroom topping. Pass shrimp-mushroom topping at the table to spoon over waffles. Makes about 10 4-inch-square waffles.

Shrimp-mushroom topping. In a large frying pan over medium heat, melt 5 tablespoons **butter** or margarine. Add 1 pound **mushrooms** (sliced) and ¼ cup chopped **parsley**; cook for about 10 minutes or until mushrooms are limp. Stir in 2 teaspoons **caraway seed**; 1 teaspoon **salt**; 1 pound medium-size cooked **shrimp** (shelled and deveined); and ¼ cup **dry sherry.** Cook over medium heat for 1 minute or until heated through. Stir together 2 teaspoons **all-purpose flour** and 2 cups **sour cream**; add to shrimp mixture just before serving and heat just until heated through. Place in serving bowl and pass at the table.

Hawaiian French Toast

Crushed pineapple included in the egg batter gives these French toast slices their delicate flavor. With a dusting of powdered sugar and a sprinkling of shredded coconut, they are sweet enough to eat as is — without the addition of syrup or jam.

(Continued on next page)

Seasoning your griddle or iron

If your pancake griddle (range-top or electric) or waffle iron (aebleskiver, heart-shaped, Belgian, or other range-top or electric) is new and not fluorocarbon coated, it may require seasoning to prevent batter from sticking.

To season, preheat iron or griddle to medium-hot—until water dripped onto the surface sizzles. Brush entire cooking surface—grids, cups, and flat surfaces—amply with salad oil. Continue to heat (close waffle iron) just until oil smokes, then remove from heat and let cool completely (open waffle iron to cool). Wipe clean and your iron is ready to use.

If you have an old iron or griddle that seems to stick, wash all cooking surfaces in soapy water. (For electrical appliances, be sure to check manufacturer's instructions to determine which parts can be submerged in water.) Then season as directed above.

4 eggs
1 teaspoon vanilla
1 tablespoon *each* maple-flavored syrup (page 52 or purchased), sour cream, and granulated sugar
1 can (about 8 oz.) crushed pineapple, drained
¼ cup milk
8 slices day-old bread, crusts trimmed (if desired)
About 6 tablespoons butter or margarine
Powdered sugar
Shredded coconut

In a blender, whirl eggs, vanilla, syrup, sour cream, granulated sugar, pineapple, and milk until smooth. (Or place in a large bowl and beat with an electric beater.)

Cut bread slices diagonally in half and arrange in a large shallow dish. Pour egg-pineapple mixture over bread; briefly, then turn to coat other side.

In a large frying pan, over medium heat, melt about 2 tablespoons of the butter. Place a few pieces of soaked bread in pan and cook until browned on the bottom. Turn and brown other side. Use remaining butter as needed. Remove to a warm platter and keep warm in a 200° oven until all bread has been cooked. Dust with powdered sugar and sprinkle with shredded coconut. Makes 4 servings of 4 slices each.

Freezer French Toast

Thick slices of French bread soak up an egg-nutmeg batter before they're frozen for a convenient freezer-to-oven-to-table entrée. You bake (without thawing) as many slices as you want. Serve topped with powdered sugar, honey, or syrup.

4 eggs
1 cup milk
2 tablespoons sugar
1 teaspoon vanilla
¼ teaspoon ground nutmeg
8 slices day-old French bread, cut ¾ inch thick
Butter or margarine, melted

In a medium-size bowl, beat together eggs, milk, sugar, vanilla, and nutmeg. Place bread slices on a rimmed baking sheet. Pour egg mixture over bread and let stand for a few minutes. Turn slices over and let stand until all the egg mixture is absorbed. Freeze, uncovered, until firm; then package airtight and return to freezer.

To serve, place desired number of frozen slices on a lightly greased baking sheet. Brush each slice with melted butter. Bake in a 500° oven for 8 minutes. Turn slices over, brush with melted butter; bake an additional 10 minutes or until nicely browned. Makes 4 servings of 2 slices each.

Sausage & Apricot-topped French Toast

(Pictured on opposite page)

In this recipe, day-old French bread soaks up a spicy egg batter and then is fried until golden and puffy. Over each slice go warm sausages and apricots and then a dollop of cool sour cream. Any leftover slices can be frozen, packaged airtight, and recrisped in a preheated 400° oven for 7 to 10 minutes.

1 pound precooked pork sausage links
1 pound apricots, halved and pitted, or 1 can (1 lb. 14 oz.) apricot halves, drained
3 tablespoons firmly packed brown sugar
6 eggs
½ cup baking mix (biscuit mix)
2 tablespoons sugar
½ teaspoon ground cinnamon
1½ cups milk
1 loaf (about 1 lb.) day-old French bread
Salad oil
Sour cream

In a frying pan over medium-high heat, brown sausage links on all sides; push to one side of pan and discard all but 2 tablespoons of the drippings. To drippings, add apricots and brown sugar; stir just until sugar dissolves and apricots look glazed. Mix with sausages and keep warm while making French toast.

In a medium-size bowl, beat eggs. Blend in baking mix, sugar, cinnamon, and milk; mix until smooth. Cut bread into 1-inch-thick slices; soak slices in batter, a few at a time, turning once, until all are completely saturated.

In a wide frying pan over medium heat, add about ¼ inch oil. When oil is hot, add a few bread slices at a time. Cover and cook for 5 minutes or until browned and slightly puffy; turn and brown other side. Drain on paper towels; keep warm. Repeat until all slices have been cooked. Put sausages and apricots in a serving bowl to pass at the table. Pass another bowl filled with sour cream to spoon on each toast slice. Makes about 6 servings of 2 slices each.

FRENCH TOAST WITH A CONTINENTAL FLAIR sports a toothsome topping of spicy sausage and tangy glazed apricots. The recipe is above.

Breads, Muffins, Coffee Cakes & other baker's delights

A bounty of baker's delights awaits you in this chapter: glorious sweet coffee cakes and doughnuts, buttery-rich rolls, flaky puff pastries with plump fruit perched on top, and hearty and nutritious muffins and breads. There's something for everyone.

Some are plain, perfect for a family breakfast; others are fancy enough for holiday fare. Some can be stirred up in minutes; others, made with a bubbly sponge of yeast, require time and a gentle hand. Whatever your choice, your breakfasts and brunches will be enhanced with the addition of freshly baked breads or pastries, and their aroma in your home will pleasantly reveal their presence.

Brunch Corn Bread

High and light, moist and tender — with a hint of sweetness—this corn bread is sure to become one of your favorites. Spread hot squares lavishly with honey butter (page 52), if desired.

- 1 cup *each* baking mix (biscuit mix) and yellow cornmeal
- 3 teaspoons baking powder
- 2 eggs
- 1 cup milk
- ⅓ cup honey
- 4 tablespoons butter or margarine, melted and cooled
  Honey butter (page 52), optional

In a large bowl, stir together baking mix, cornmeal, and baking powder. In a small bowl, beat eggs lightly; stir in milk, honey, and butter. Pour egg mixture into dry ingredients and mix just until moistened.

Turn batter into a well-greased 8-inch-square baking pan. Bake in a 400° oven for 25 to 30 minutes or until a wooden skewer inserted in center comes out clean. Cut into squares and serve warm with honey butter, if desired. Makes about 9 servings.

Raisin-Nut Honey Bread

Laden with raisins and nuts, this honey-sweetened bread is delicious spread with butter, soft cream cheese, or breakfast cheese.

- ½ cup (¼ lb.) butter or margarine, softened
- ½ cup firmly packed brown sugar
- 2 eggs
- ½ cup *each* honey and buttermilk
- 2 cups all-purpose flour
- 1 teaspoon soda
- ½ teaspoons *each* ground ginger and ground cloves
- 2 teaspoons ground cinnamon
- ¼ teaspoon salt
- ½ cup *each* raisins and chopped walnuts

In a large bowl, beat together butter and sugar until smoothly blended. Add eggs, one at a time, and beat until fluffy. Blend in honey and buttermilk. In a separate bowl, stir together flour, soda, ginger, cloves, cinnamon, and salt until thoroughly blended; mix into butter mixture. Stir in raisins and nuts. Spoon batter into a greased 9 by 5-inch loaf pan.

Bake in a 325° oven for 1 hour or until bread begins to pull away from sides of pan and a wooden skewer inserted in center comes out clean. Let cool in pan for 10 minutes, then turn out onto a rack to cool completely before slicing. Makes 1 loaf.

Graham Yogurt Bread

(Pictured on page 11)

Here is a nutritious, even-textured bread that bakes in three 1-pound vegetable or fruit cans (*not* coffee cans). Tightly wrapped and stored in the refrigerator, these loaves stay fresh for about 5 days.

    2 cups graham flour or whole wheat flour
    ½ cup all-purpose flour
    2 teaspoons soda
    1 teaspoon salt
    2 cups unflavored yogurt
    ½ cup molasses
    1 cup raisins
    ½ cup chopped walnuts

Remove one end from each of the three 1-pound cans; rinse cans, dry, and grease well. In a large bowl, stir together graham flour, all-purpose flour, soda, and salt until thoroughly blended. Stir in yogurt, molasses, raisins, and walnuts; mix well. Divide batter evenly into cans.

Bake in a 350° oven for about 1 hour or until a wooden skewer inserted in center comes out clean. Cool in cans for about 10 minutes; then turn out and stand loaves upright on a rack to cool completely. Makes 3 small loaves.

Cinnamon Swirl Loaf

(Pictured on page 62)

Light, tender, fine texture, and a touch of sweetness characterizes this cinnamon swirl yeast bread made with an electric mixer. Serve it warm or cooled, spread with butter or jam. For a quick morning treat, try it sliced, toasted, and spread with peanut butter.

    1   package active dry yeast
    ¼   cup warm water (about 110°)
    ⅔   cup milk (about 110°)
    1   teaspoon salt
    ½   cup granulated sugar
    ½   cup (¼ lb.) butter or margarine, melted and cooled
    2   eggs
    3   to 3½ cups all-purpose flour
    1½ teaspoons ground cinnamon
    ½   cup powdered sugar, unsifted
    ½   teaspoon orange or vanilla extract
    1   tablespoon milk

In a large bowl, combine yeast and water; let stand until bubbly. Stir in milk, salt, and ¼ cup *each* of the granulated sugar and butter. Add eggs and 1½ cups of the flour; beat until smooth. Then beat in 1½ cups of the remaining flour until smooth.

Turn dough over in greased bowl; cover and let rise in a warm place until doubled (about 1 hour). Turn dough out onto a floured board and knead lightly, adding more flour as needed.

Roll out into a 9 by 18-inch rectangle. Brush with 2 tablespoons of the remaining butter. Mix the remaining ¼ cup granulated sugar with cinnamon; sprinkle over dough.

Starting at narrow end, roll up tightly. Turn loaf over and pinch a seam down the center. Put shaped loaf into a greased 9 by 5-inch loaf pan. Brush top with the remaining 2 tablespoons butter; cover and let rise until almost doubled (about 45 minutes).

Bake in a 350° oven for about 30 to 35 minutes or until loaf is nicely browned and sounds hollow when tapped. Turn loaf out of pan onto a rack. Stir together powdered sugar, extract, and the 1 tablespoon milk. While bread is still warm, drizzle icing over top and let it run down the sides. Cool before slicing or wrapping. Makes 1 loaf.

Moist Banana Bread

The delicate flavor of ripe bananas makes this bread rich-tasting, moist, and tender. Wrapped and refrigerated, it stays moist for a week; freeze for longer storage. Serve slices spread with butter.

    1½ cups all-purpose flour
    1   teaspoon *each* salt and soda
    1   cup mashed ripe bananas (about 3)
    1   cup sugar
    1   egg
    ¼   cup butter or margarine, melted and cooled

In a bowl, stir together flour, salt and soda; set aside. In another bowl, combine bananas and sugar; stir well. Then add egg and butter and stir to blend. Pour liquid ingredients into dry ingredients and mix just until moistened. Pour batter into a greased 8½ by 4½-inch loaf pan.

Bake in a 325° oven for about 55 to 60 minutes or until bread begins to pull away from sides of pan and a wooden skewer inserted in center comes out clean. Let cool in pan for 10 minutes, then turn out onto a rack to cool completely before slicing. Makes 1 loaf.

Ready-bake Bran Muffins

These wholesome, almost cakelike muffins are made from a fruit-laced batter that will keep in the refrigerator for several weeks. You use only enough batter to make the number of muffins you want, and they bake light and tender while the coffee brews.

(Continued on page 63)

3 cups whole bran cereal
1 cup boiling water
2 eggs, lightly beaten
2 cups buttermilk
½ cup salad oil
1 cup raisins, currants, chopped pitted dates,
    or chopped pitted prunes
2½ teaspoons soda
½ teaspoon salt
1 cup sugar
2½ cups all-purpose flour

In a large bowl, combine cereal with boiling water, stirring to moisten. Set aside until cool, then add eggs, buttermilk, oil, and fruit; blend well. Mix together the soda, salt, sugar, and flour; then stir in the bran mixture. (At this point you may cover and refrigerate in a tightly covered container for as long as two weeks, baking muffins at your convenience; stir batter to evenly distribute fruit before using.)

To bake, spoon batter into greased 2½-inch-diameter muffin cups. (Fill each cup ⅔ to ¾ full.) Bake in a 425° oven for about 20 minutes or until tops spring back when lightly touched. Serve hot. Makes 2 to 2½ dozen muffins.

Sweet Mini-muffins

You will want to make these sweet, butter-rich morsels frequently, and have plenty on hand — they disappear quickly! They can be made ahead and frozen; but cool them thoroughly first, and cover loosely so the cinnamon-sugar coating does not dissolve.

4 tablespoons butter or margarine, softened
½ cup sugar
1 egg
2 cups all-purpose flour
4 teaspoons baking powder
½ teaspoon salt
½ teaspoon ground nutmeg
1 cup milk
    About ½ cup butter or margarine, melted
2 teaspoons ground cinnamon mixed with ½ cup
    sugar

Beat together butter and the ½ cup sugar until well blended, then beat in egg. Sift together flour, baking powder, salt, and nutmeg. Stir dry ingredients alter-

QUICK AND NOURISHING BREAKFAST TREATS teamed here are fragrant Cinnamon Swirl Bread (page 61) with a choice of toppings –Date Nut Butter (page 52) and peanut butter– and a generous glass of mellow Banana & Fruit Nectar (page 13).

nately with milk into the butter-sugar mixture and blend thoroughly. Spoon about 1 rounded teaspoon batter into each greased 1½-inch mini-muffin cup. Bake in a 375° oven for 20 minutes or until golden brown. Remove from pans. While still hot, dip each muffin entirely into melted butter, coating evenly, then roll in cinnamon-sugar mixture. Serve warm or cold. To freeze, cool thoroughly, wrap in plastic wrap, then put into plastic bags. Remove as many as you need, but do not thaw in the plastic wrap. Makes 3 dozen mini-muffins.

Sunshine Muffins

On a bright summer day or a cold winter one, these moist and nutritious muffins will highlight any meal. Wheat germ gives them a crunchy texture; orange juice and honey add a touch of sweetness.

4 tablespoons butter or margarine, softened
¼ cup honey
1 egg, lightly beaten
1 teaspoon grated orange peel
½ cup orange juice
1 cup all-purpose flour
1 teaspoon baking powder
½ teaspoon salt
¼ teaspoon soda
½ cup wheat germ

In a small bowl, blend butter and honey. Add egg, grated orange peel, and orange juice; blend thoroughly. In a separate bowl, stir together flour, baking powder, salt, soda, and wheat germ. Make a well in center of flour mixture; add liquid ingredients all at once, stir just to moisten. Spoon into well-greased 2½-inch muffin cups, filling each two-thirds full.

Bake in a 375° oven for about 20 minutes or until browned and tops spring back when lightly touched. Makes 1 dozen muffins.

Crumpets

Crumpets have holes for a reason. How else, ask the British, can a generous amount of butter properly permeate each moist and springy bite?

Best described as a cross between an English muffin and a pancake, crumpets are served warm — either freshly baked or toasted — with butter and jam, marmalade, or honey.

English cooks use 3½-inch metal crumpet rings to contain the simple yeast batter while it bakes in a frying pan or on a griddle. You can use 3-inch flan rings or round, open-topped cooky cutters; or you can even use tuna cans with the tops and bottoms removed.

 1 package active dry yeast
 1 teaspoon sugar
 ¼ cup warm water (about 110°)
 ⅓ cup milk, at room temperature
 1 egg
   About 4 tablespoons butter or margarine, melted
 1 cup all-purpose flour
 ½ teaspoon salt

In a large bowl, combine yeast, sugar, and water; let stand until bubbly (about 15 minutes). Blend in milk, egg, and 1 tablespoon of the melted butter. Add flour and salt and beat until smooth. Cover and let stand in a warm place until almost doubled (about 45 minutes).

Brush bottom of a heavy frying pan or griddle and the inside of each ring with butter. Heat rings in pan over low heat; pour about 3 tablespoons batter into each. Bake for about 7 minutes or until holes appear and tops are dry. Remove rings and turn crumpets to brown other side lightly (about 2 minutes). Repeat with remaining batter.

Serve warm, or cool on a rack and toast just before serving. Makes 7 or 8 crumpets.

Buttermilk Scone Hearts

Studded with fruit, these buttery, heart-shaped scones are sure to please any valentine on the morning of February 14. In fact, they go together so quickly, you can sneak out of bed a little early and present them any day as a breakfast surprise.

 3 cups all-purpose flour
 ⅓ cup sugar
 2½ teaspoons baking powder
 ½ teaspoon soda
 ¾ teaspoon salt
 ¾ cup firm butter or margarine, cut in small pieces
 ¾ cup chopped pitted dates or currants
 1 teaspoon grated orange peel
 1 cup buttermilk
   About 1 tablespoon cream or milk
 ¼ teaspoon ground cinnamon mixed with 2 tablespoons sugar

In a large bowl, stir together flour, sugar, baking powder, soda, and salt until thoroughly blended. Using a pastry blender or 2 knives, cut butter into flour mixture until it resembles coarse cornmeal; stir in dates and orange peel. Make a well in the center of the butter-flour mixture; add buttermilk all at once. Stir mixture with a fork until dough cleans the sides of the bowl.

With your hands, gather dough into a ball; turn out onto a lightly floured board. Roll or pat into a ½-inch-thick circle. Using a 2½-inch heart (or other shape) cutter, cut into individual scones. Place 1½ inches apart on lightly greased baking sheets. Brush tops of scones with cream; sprinkle lightly with cinnamon-sugar mixture.

Bake in a 425° oven for 12 minutes or until tops are lightly browned. Serve warm. Makes about 18 scones.

Popovers

These fragile shells are nothing but crisp golden crusts and air. You can bake them in your choice of containers: shiny, lightweight metal muffin pans; dark, heavy cast-iron popover pans; or ovenproof glass custard cups. But once they're in the oven, no peeking or they'll fall flat! Lavish these light hollow muffins with butter and preserves or fill them with a creamy entrée.

 1 cup all-purpose flour
 ¼ teaspoon salt
 1 teaspoon sugar (optional)
 1 tablespoon melted butter or margarine, or salad oil
 1 cup milk
 2 large eggs

In a bowl, stir together flour, salt, and sugar (if used) until thoroughly blended. Add butter, milk, and eggs; beat until very smooth (about 2½ minutes), scraping bowl frequently with a rubber spatula. Pour into greased containers (see choices above), filling each about one-half full. If using greased ovenproof glass cups, batter will yield 12 popovers, ⅓-cup size; 10 popovers, ½-cup size; or 8 or 9 popovers, 6-ounce size.

For a richly browned shell with fairly moist interior, bake on center rack in a 400° oven for about 40 minutes or until well browned and firm to touch. For a lighter-colored popover, drier inside, bake in a 375° oven for 50 to 55 minutes. (Keep oven door closed; popovers may collapse if a draft of air hits them just as they are swelling above the cup. Remove from pans and serve hot. Makes 8 to 12 popovers.

If you like your popovers especially dry inside, loosen them from pan but leave sitting at an angle in cups; prick side of each popover with a skewer and let stand in the turned-off oven, door slightly ajar, for 8 to 10 minutes.

Cheese-Egg Puffs

These golden crisp cream puffs with airy moist centers are laced with melted cheese. Though best served hot from the oven, they can be made a day ahead and reheated. Break them open and generously spread with butter, or gently cut off their tops and fill the hollows with your favorite creamed entrée. For a large group, you can double the recipe or make the puffs smaller.

½ cup milk
2 tablespoons butter or margarine
¼ teaspoon salt
   Dash of pepper
½ cup all-purpose flour
2 eggs
½ cup shredded Swiss or Cheddar cheese

In a 1½-quart pan, combine milk, butter, salt, and pepper. Bring to a full boil over medium heat. Add flour all at once and stir until mixture leaves sides of pan and forms a ball. Remove from heat and beat in eggs, one at a time, until mixture is smooth and well blended. Beat in ⅓ cup of the shredded cheese.

Using 2 large spoons, make 4 equal mounds of dough, and place 2 inches apart on a greased baking sheet. Sprinkle the remaining cheese evenly over the mounds. Bake in a 375° oven for 30 to 35 minutes or until puffs are well browned and crisp. Serve hot, or let cool on a rack and package airtight. To reheat, place puffs on a greased baking sheet and bake in a 325° oven for about 10 minutes. Makes 4 puffs.

Quick Sourdough Biscuits

Substituting sourdough starter (page 68) for some of the liquid and flour in a standard baking powder biscuit recipe makes for fluffy, moist biscuits with a tangy, sour flavor.

1 cup all-purpose flour
1 tablespoon baking powder
½ teaspoon *each* salt, soda, and sugar
¼ cup shortening
1 cup sourdough starter (page 68)
   About 2 tablespoons butter or margarine, melted

In a mixing bowl, stir together flour, baking powder, salt, soda, and sugar. Using a pastry blender or two knives, cut shortening into flour mixture until fine crumbs form. Stir in starter until a soft dough forms and cleans the sides of the bowl.

With your hands, gather dough into a ball and gently knead in bowl for about 30 seconds. On a lightly floured board, roll dough into a ½-inch-thick circle; cut dough into biscuits with a 2-inch-round cutter. Place biscuits 2 inches apart on ungreased baking sheets, lightly brush tops with melted butter, and let rest for 15 minutes. Bake in a 425° oven for 12 minutes or until tops are golden brown. Makes about 16 biscuits.

Cinnamon-raisin biscuits. Follow directions for quick sourdough biscuits above, but increase **sugar** to ¼ cup and add ¾ teaspoon **ground cinnamon** and ¼ teaspoon **ground nutmeg** to flour mixture before cutting in shortening. Stir in ⅓ cup **raisins** or currants with the sourdough starter.

Sticky Pecan Rolls

Here are sweet yeast rolls that need only one rising before they are baked. Let them cool for at least 10 minutes before handling — the caramel pecan topping will be very hot.

¼ teaspoon soda
¼ cup granulated sugar
1 teaspoon salt
1 package active dry yeast
2½ to 3 cups all-purpose flour
1 cup buttermilk
3 tablespoons salad oil
2 tablespoons water
4 tablespoons butter or margarine, melted
½ cup *each* firmly packed brown sugar and pecan halves
1 teaspoon ground cinnamon

In a large bowl, combine soda, granulated sugar, salt, yeast, and 1 cup of the flour. Place buttermilk and oil in a pan over medium-low heat until warm (120°); add to flour mixture and beat for about 2 minutes. Stir in 1½ cups of the remaining flour and beat until smooth. Turn dough out onto a floured board and knead until smooth and elastic (8 to 10 minutes), adding more flour as needed. Let dough rest on board while preparing pan.

(Continued on next page)

Combine water, 2 tablespoons of the melted butter, and ¼ cup of the brown sugar. Distribute mixture equally among 12 2½-inch muffin cups; top mixture with pecans.

Roll dough into a 12 by 15-inch rectangle. Brush surface with the remaining 2 tablespoons butter. Mix together the remaining ¼ cup brown sugar and cinnamon; sprinkle evenly over buttered dough. Starting with narrow end, roll lengthwise into a cylinder, cut in 12 equal slices, and place, cut side down, in muffin cups. Let rise, uncovered, in a warm place until doubled (about 1½ hours). Bake in a 350° oven for about 25 minutes or until tops are golden. Invert immediately onto a serving plate; let pan rest briefly on rolls so syrup can drizzle over them. Let cool for 10 minutes before serving. Makes 1 dozen rolls.

Brioches

(Pictured on opposite page)

French brioches come in different shapes and sizes; here we offer you the petite brioche (little brioche). You mix the soft yeast dough a day in advance, then let it rest overnight in the refrigerator. This makes the dough springy and easy to shape.

> 1 **package active dry yeast**
> ½ **cup warm water (about 110°)**
> 2 **teaspoons sugar**
> 1¼ **teaspoons salt**
> 3 **eggs**
> ¼ **cup butter or margarine, softened**
> 3½ **to 4 cups all-purpose flour**
> 1 **egg yolk beaten with 1 tablespoon milk**

In a large bowl, dissolve yeast in water; let stand until bubbly. Stir in sugar, salt, and eggs. Cut butter into small pieces and add to liquid. Gradually beat in 3½ cups flour, mixing until flour is evenly moistened and dough holds together. Shape into a ball and place on a floured board. Knead until smooth and satiny (5 to 20 minutes), adding flour as needed to prevent sticking.

Turn dough over in a greased bowl; cover and let rise in a warm place until doubled (1 to 2 hours). Punch dough down; knead briefly on a lightly floured board. Return to greased bowl; turn over to grease top. Cover with plastic wrap and refrigerate for 12 to 24 hours.

Knead on a lightly floured board to release air. Divide dough into 24 equal pieces. Dough is easiest to handle if kept cold, so shape a few at a time, keeping remaining pieces covered separately and refrigerated until ready to use.

Pinch off about ⅛ of each portion and set aside. Carefully shape each larger section into a smooth ball

by pulling surface of dough to underside of ball; this is very important if you want to achieve a good-looking brioche. Set each ball, smooth side up, in a well-buttered 3 to 4-inch petite brioche pan, fluted tart pan, or 3-inch muffin cup. Press dough down to fill pan bottom evenly. Shape small piece of dough into a teardrop that is smooth on top.

With your finger, poke a hole in center of brioche dough in pan and insert pointed end of small piece in hole, settling securely (otherwise, topknot will pop off at an angle while baking). Repeat until all brioches are shaped. If you work quickly, you can leave pans at room temperature when filled; otherwise, place each filled pan, lightly covered, in the refrigerator.

When all pans are filled, cover and let stand in a warm place until almost doubled (1 to 2 hours). With a soft brush, paint tops of brioches with egg yolk and milk mixture (do not let glaze accumulate in joint of topknot).

Bake in a 425° oven for about 20 minutes or until richly browned. Remove from pans and serve warm, or let cool on racks. Makes 24 petite brioches.

Banana Coffee Ring

(Pictured on page 27)

Packaged baking mix makes this delicious ring-shaped banana coffee cake quick and easy to assemble. While it bakes you can put the rest of the meal together.

> ½ **cup butter or margarine, melted**
> ½ **cup *each* firmly packed brown sugar and sliced almonds**
> 1 **egg**
> ¾ **cup mashed banana (about 2 bananas)**
> 3 **tablespoons granulated sugar**
> 2 **cups baking mix (biscuit mix)**
> ⅓ **cup milk**
> 1½ **teaspoons ground cinnamon**
> ½ **teaspoon ground nutmeg**

Lightly grease the sides of a 6½ to 8-cup ring mold. Pour ¼ cup of the melted butter into bottom of mold. Sprinkle half of the brown sugar and almonds over butter.

In a medium-size bowl, beat egg; add mashed banana, granulated sugar, baking mix, and milk; beat

(Continued on page 68)

HIGH AND HANDSOME BRIOCHES (recipe at left) are hollowed to hold Creamy Ham with Artichokes & Mushrooms (page 89) for this special garden brunch. Accompany with simple garnishes of carrot curls, watercress, and radish roses. And for a sweet dessert, offer bakery petit fours and tea.

...*Banana Coffee Ring (cont'd.)*

until smooth. In another bowl, stir together the remaining half of the brown sugar and almonds; mix in cinnamon and nutmeg; set aside.

Spoon half the banana batter into the mold and top with brown sugar and nut mixture. Drizzle remaining ¼ cup butter over it. Spoon the remaining batter on top and smooth with a spoon.

Bake in a 400° oven for 25 minutes or until a wooden pick inserted in center comes out clean. Immediately invert on a serving plate; let pan rest briefly on cake so syrup can drizzle over it. Cool slightly before serving. Makes 10 to 12 servings.

Quick Butter Croissants

(Pictured on page 6)

Here is a remarkably simple method of making croissants that closely resemble the traditional ones the French serve for breakfast. You cut firm butter into flour, then blend the mixture with a yeast batter. The resulting dough is marbled with pockets of butter that form flaky layers when the croissants are baked. Best of all, you can store the dough in the refrigerator (up to 4 days) until you're ready to shape and bake the rolls.

    1 package active dry yeast
    1 cup warm water (about 110°)
    ¾ cup evaporated milk
 1½ teaspoons salt
    ⅓ cup sugar
    1 egg
       About 5½ cups all-purpose flour
    4 tablespoons butter or margarine, melted and cooled
    1 cup (½ lb.) very firm butter or margarine
    1 egg beaten with 1 tablespoon water

In a large bowl, dissolve yeast in water; let stand until bubbly. Add milk, salt, sugar, egg, and 1 cup of the flour. Beat to make a smooth batter, then blend in melted butter; set aside.

In a large bowl, using a pastry blender or 2 knives, cut the 1 cup firm butter into 4 cups of the remaining flour until butter particles are the size of small peas. Pour yeast batter over top and carefully turn mixture over with a spatula to blend just until all flour is

Sourdough starter

The characteristic flavor of sourdough is not due to yeast, but to the presence of a harmless bacteria naturally present in raw milk, aged Cheddar cheese, cultured buttermilk, and yogurt. We tried making starters with all of these products and decided yogurt was the easiest to work with. But within the first 6 months, you'll have more success with your new sourdough starter if you use it in recipes that also include yeast.

Start with a 1½-quart container —glass, pottery, rigid plastic, or stainless steel. Warm the container by letting hot water stand in it for several minutes; then wipe dry.

Heat 1 cup **skim or low-fat milk** to 90°–100°F. Remove from heat; stir in 3 tablespoons unflavored, **low-fat yogurt.** Pour milk mixture into warm container, cover tightly; let stand in a warm (80°–100°) place —on top of a water heater, near the burner of a gas range (not on it), or atop a built-in refrigerator (if there's room).

Within 18 to 24 hours, starter should be about the consistency of yogurt (a curd forms and mixture does not flow readily when container is slightly tilted). If a clear liquid rises to top of milk, stir it back in; but if liquid has turned light pink, it indicates that milk is beginning to break down, so discard and start over.

After a curd has formed, gradually stir 1 cup **all-purpose flour** into starter until smoothly blended. Cover tightly and let stand in a warm place (80°–100°) until mixture is full of bubbles and has a sour smell; this takes 2 to 5 days. If clear liquid forms during this time, stir it back into starter. But if liquid turns pink, discard all but ¼ cup of starter. Blend in a mixture of 1 cup *each* warm **milk** (90°–100°) and **all-purpose flour.** Cover tightly and let stand again in warm place until bubbly — then it's ready to use. Or cover and store in refrigerator. This makes 1½ cups starter.

Always let your starter warm to room temperature before using (this takes about 4 to 6 hours). You can leave it out overnight to use first thing in the morning.

To maintain an ample supply, each time you use part of your starter, replenish it with equal amounts of warm **milk** (90°–100°) and **all-purpose flour.** (If you use ½ cup starter, blend in a mixture of ½ cup *each* warm milk and all-purpose flour.) Cover and let stand in a warm place for several hours or overnight, until it is again full of bubbles; then store in the refrigerator.

moistened. Cover with plastic wrap and refrigerate for at least 4 hours or up to 4 days.

Turn dough out onto a lightly floured board, press into a compact ball, and knead briefly to release air. Divide dough into 4 equal parts. Shape 1 part at a time, leaving remaining dough (wrapped in plastic wrap) in refrigerator.

On a floured board, roll 1 part of dough into a 14-inch circle, adding flour as needed to prevent sticking. Using a sharp knife, cut circle into 8 equal wedges.

Loosely roll each wedge from wide end toward point. Shape into a crescent and place, point side down, on an ungreased baking sheet. Repeat until all croissants are shaped and placed, 1½ inches apart all around, on ungreased baking sheets. Cover lightly and let rise at room temperature in a draft-free place. (Do not speed rising by placing in a warm spot.)

When almost doubled (about 2 hours), brush with egg-water mixture. Bake in a 325° oven for about 35 minutes or until lightly browned. Serve warm, or let cool on racks. Makes 32 croissants.

Hot Cross Buns

Though breads have been decorated with crosses since ancient times, the custom of serving hot cross buns at Easter probably began in 14th century England. According to legend, a kind-hearted monk baked them on Good Friday to feed the poor. As his gesture evolved into a seasonal tradition, many people believed the little breads contained sacred powers of protection.

    1   package active dry yeast
    ¼   cup warm water (about 110°)
    1   cup warm milk (about 110°)
    2   tablespoons butter or margarine
    ⅓   cup sugar
    ¾   teaspoon *each* salt and ground cinnamon
    ¼   teaspoon *each* ground cloves and ground nutmeg
    2   eggs
    ¾   cup currants
    ¼   cup finely diced candied orange peel or citron
        About 4½ cups all-purpose flour
    1   egg yolk beaten with 1 tablespoon water
        Lemon frosting (recipe follows)

In a bowl, dissolve yeast in water; let stand until bubbly. Stir in milk, butter, sugar, salt, cinnamon, cloves, and nutmeg. Beat in eggs. Stir in currants, orange peel, and enough of the flour (about 4 cups) to make a soft dough.

Turn dough out onto a floured board; knead until smooth and satiny (10 to 20 minutes), adding flour as needed to prevent sticking. Turn dough over in a

greased bowl; cover and let rise in a warm place until doubled (about 1½ hours).

Punch dough down and divide into 36 equal pieces; shape each into a smooth ball. Place balls about 2 inches apart on lightly greased baking sheets. Brush each gently with egg yolk mixture. Cover lightly and let rise in a warm place until doubled (about 35 minutes).

Bake in a 400° oven for about 10 minutes or until lightly browned. Cool on racks for about 5 minutes. Prepare lemon frosting and, with a spoon or the tip of a knife, drizzle frosting over top of each bun to make a small cross. Makes 3 dozen buns.

Lemon frosting. Combine 1 cup sifted **powdered sugar,** 2 teaspoons **lemon juice,** and 1 teaspoon **water;** beat until smooth.

Orange Biscuit Pinwheels

These quick and easy orange-glazed rolls are made from biscuit dough instead of yeast dough. You can build a meal around them by adding sausage links, scrambled eggs, and fresh fruit slices to the menu.

        Orange syrup (directions follow)
    2   cups all-purpose flour
    1   tablespoon baking powder
    ½   teaspoon salt
    ¼   cup solid shortening
    ¾   cup milk
    2   tablespoons butter or margarine, melted
    ¼   cup sugar
    ½   teaspoon ground cinnamon

Prepare orange syrup and pour into a round 8 or 9-inch baking pan; let cool while preparing biscuit dough.

In a medium-size bowl, combine flour, baking

(Continued on page 71)

powder, and salt. With a pastry blender or 2 knives cut in shortening until fine crumbs form. Stir in milk. On a lightly floured board gently knead dough 20 to 25 times. Roll dough into a 10 by 13-inch rectangle. Brush surface with melted butter. Stir together sugar and cinnamon; sprinkle evenly over buttered dough.

Starting with narrow end, roll lengthwise into a cylinder. Cut into 10 equal slices and arrange, slightly apart and cut side down, over syrup in pan. Bake in a 425° oven for 30 minutes or until tops are browned. Invert immediately onto a serving plate; let pan rest briefly on rolls so syrup can drizzle over them. Serve warm. Makes 10 rolls.

Orange syrup. In a pan, combine 3 tablespoons **butter or margarine,** 1/3 cup *each* **sugar** and **orange juice,** and 1½ teaspoons **grated orange peel.** Boil gently over medium heat, uncovered, for about 3 minutes or until syrup thickens slightly and is reduced to 2/3 cup.

Fresh Apple Coffee Cake

(Pictured on opposite page)

Fresh apples make this coffee cake moist and tender. Serve warm or cooled with a dusting of powdered sugar. Use golden or red delicious apples.

    1 cup all-purpose flour
    ½ teaspoon salt
    1 teaspoon soda
    2 cups cored, peeled, and diced sweet apple
    1 egg
    ¼ cup salad oil
    1 cup sugar
    1 teaspoon ground cinnamon
    ¼ teaspoon ground nutmeg
    ½ cup chopped nuts

Sift flour, salt, and soda together; set aside. Place apple in a medium-size bowl. Break egg over apples. Add oil, sugar, cinnamon, nutmeg, and nuts; blend thoroughly. Stir dry mixture into apple mixture just until flour is moist. (The mixture will seem dry.) Spread in a greased 8-inch-square baking pan. Bake in a 350° oven for 40 to 45 minutes, or until a wooden pick inserted in center comes out clean. Let stand in pan for 10 minutes before turning out on a wire rack. Makes 9 servings.

FRESH APPLE COFFEE CAKE (recipe above) is moist, fragrant with cinnamon, and chockfull of sweet apple morsels.

Cottage Cheese Pan Rolls

The dough for these speedy, light yeast rolls needs only one rising. For a flavor variation, add 2 teaspoons dill weed to the cottage cheese.

    1 package active dry yeast
    ½ cup warm water (about 110°)
    ½ pint cottage cheese
    1 egg
    2 teaspoons baking powder
    ¼ teaspoon soda
    1 teaspoon salt
    1 tablespoon sugar
       About 3¾ cups all-purpose flour
    2 tablespoons firm butter or margarine

In a small bowl, dissolve yeast in water; let stand until bubbly. In a blender, combine cottage cheese and egg; whirl until smooth.

In a large bowl, stir together baking powder, soda, salt, sugar, and 3¼ cups of the flour. Work butter into flour mixture with your fingers until no large particles remain. Stir in cheese mixture, then yeast mixture.

Turn dough out onto a floured board and knead until smooth and satiny (5 to 20 minutes), adding flour as needed to prevent sticking. Turn dough over in a greased bowl; cover and let rise in a warm place for about 30 minutes.

Punch dough down and divide into 18 equal pieces; shape each piece into a smooth ball. Arrange balls in 2 greased 8-inch-round baking pans. Cover lightly and let stand for 10 minutes.

Bake in a 350° oven for about 25 minutes or until golden. Cool on racks. Makes 1½ dozen rolls.

Buttermilk Coffee Cake

This sweet, moist, tender cake with a crunchy nut topping can be served from its own baking pan right out of the oven.

    2¼ cups all-purpose flour
    ½   teaspoon *each* salt and ground cinnamon
    1   cup firmly packed brown sugar
    ¾   cup *each* granulated sugar and salad oil
    ½   cup coarsely chopped walnuts
    1¼ teaspoons ground cinnamon
    1   teaspoon *each* soda and baking powder
    1   egg
    1   cup buttermilk

In a medium-size bowl, mix together flour, salt, the ½ teaspoon cinnamon, brown sugar, granulated sugar, and salad oil. Beat with an electric mixer on medium speed until well blended. Remove ¾ cup of this mixture for the topping and blend into it the nuts and the 1¼ teaspoons cinnamon; set aside.

To the remaining mixture, add soda, baking powder, egg, and buttermilk; blend until smooth. Pour mixture into a greased 9 by 13-inch baking pan; smooth the top with the back of a spoon. Evenly spoon the reserved topping over batter and lightly press it in with the back of a spoon. Bake in a 350° oven for 25 to 30 minutes or until a wooden pick inserted in center comes out clean. Cut into squares. Makes about 12 servings.

Pineapple Upside-down Cake

Good for breakfast or brunch, this quick-to-make coffee cake is sure to become one of your favorites. Serve it warm, just out of the oven, or cooled.

    4 tablespoons butter or margarine
    ½ cup firmly packed brown sugar
    1 can (about 1 lb. 4 oz.) sliced pineapple in syrup
    1 cup all-purpose flour
    1 teaspoon baking powder
    ¼ teaspoon salt
    3 eggs
    1 cup granulated sugar

In a heavy 10-inch frying pan with an ovenproof handle, melt butter over medium-low heat. Add brown sugar and cook, stirring constantly, for about 10 minutes or until bubbly. Remove pan from heat. Drain pineapple and reserve ¼ cup of the syrup. Place pineapple slices in a single layer atop sugar-butter mixture; set aside to cool.

Meanwhile, in a small bowl, combine flour, baking powder, and salt; set aside. In another bowl, beat eggs with the granulated sugar until light and fluffy; add the reserved ¼ cup pineapple syrup. Fold dry ingredients into egg mixture. Pour over pineapple in frying pan. Bake, uncovered, in a 350° oven for 35 to 40 minutes or until a wooden pick inserted in center comes out clean. While still warm, loosen cake with a spatula and immediately turn out on a serving plate; let pan rest briefly on cake so syrup can drizzle over cake. Makes 6 to 8 servings.

Quick Fruit Tarts

(Pictured on page 75)

For a sweet and delicious change from toast with your morning eggs, try these easy-to-make fruit tarts quickly prepared with purchased frozen puff pastry shells. (Thaw the frozen shells in the refrigerator the night before; they take an hour to thaw at room temperature.) They're best when served fresh and crisp from the oven.

    1 package (about 10 oz.) frozen puff pastry shells, thawed
    4 cups pitted fresh cherries or about 36 fresh apricot halves (or the same amount of canned fruit, well drained)
    2 tablespoons sugar
      About ¼ teaspoon ground cardamom, ground cinnamon, or ground nutmeg
    4 tablespoons cherry or apricot jam
      Sour cream (optional)

On a lightly floured board, roll out each pastry shell to make a 6-inch circle. Place on ungreased rimmed baking sheets. Top each with about ⅔ cup cherries or 6 apricot halves; sprinkle each with 1 teaspoon sugar and a light dusting of cardamom.

Bake, uncovered, in a 400° oven for about 25 minutes or until golden brown. Spread 2 teaspoons jam over top of each to glaze. Serve warm, plain or with sour cream (if desired). Makes 6 tarts.

Swedish Cardamom Wreaths

One of the pleasures of Christmas morning, perhaps after gifts have been opened, can be sharing a loaf of warm and fragrant breakfast bread with your family. Flavored with aromatic cardamom, these braided Swedish wreaths are decorated with icing and cherries. Cutting tends to squash this tender bread, so it's best to pull it apart to eat.

    1 package active dry yeast
    ¼ cup warm water (about 110°)
    2½ cups warm milk (about 110°)
    ¾ cup butter or margarine, melted and cooled
    1 egg
    ½ teaspoon salt
    1 cup sugar
    1½ teaspoons ground cardamom
      About 7½ cups all-purpose flour
      Sugar icing (recipe follows)
      Red or green candied cherries, halved (optional)

In a large bowl, dissolve yeast in water; let stand until bubbly. Stir in milk, butter, egg, salt, sugar, and cardamom until blended.

Gradually beat in about 7 cups of the flour to form a stiff dough. Turn dough out onto a floured board; knead until smooth and satiny (10 to 20 minutes), adding flour as needed to prevent sticking. Turn dough over in a greased bowl; cover and let rise in a warm place until doubled (1½ to 2 hours).

Punch dough down and divide into 6 equal portions; roll each to form a rope about 24 inches long. Place 3 ropes on a greased baking sheet; pinch tops together and loosely braid. Curve braid to make a

wreath; pinch ends together. Repeat to make second wreath. Cover and let rise in a warm place until almost doubled (about 40 minutes).

Bake in a 350° oven for 35 to 40 minutes or until lightly browned. Cool on racks for 10 minutes. Prepare sugar icing and spoon over tops of wreaths, letting it drizzle down sides. Decorate with cherries if you wish. (If made ahead, cool completely and freeze; decorate with icing and cherries after bread is reheated.) Makes 2 large loaves.

Sugar icing. For each loaf, beat until smooth: 1 cup unsifted **powdered sugar**, 2 tablespoons **milk**, and ½ teaspoon **lemon extract**. Double recipe to make icing for 2 loaves.

Streuselkuchen

German bakers often tuck a luscious filling under the crumbly streusel topping on their pastries. This super-size version of streuselkuchen can be constructed in a pizza pan or jelly roll pan, and with a choice of three fillings. It serves a dozen or more.

- ¼ cup milk
- 2 tablespoons granulated sugar
- ¾ teaspoon salt
- ¼ cup butter or margarine
- 1 package active dry yeast
- ¼ cup warm water (about 110°)
- 2 eggs
  About 3¼ cups all-purpose flour
  Poppy seed, apple, or cheese filling (directions follow)
  Streusel topping (directions follow)
  Powdered sugar (optional)

In a small pan over medium heat, warm milk, granulated sugar, salt, and butter just until butter melts; cool to lukewarm.

In a large bowl, dissolve yeast in water; let stand until bubbly. Blend in cooled milk mixture and eggs, then add 2 cups of the flour. Beat at medium speed for 3 minutes or until batter pulls away from sides of bowl. Using a spoon, stir in 1 cup more flour to make a soft dough. Turn dough out onto a floured board; knead until smooth. Turn dough over in a greased bowl; cover and let rise in a warm place until doubled (1 to 1½ hours).

Meanwhile, prepare filling of your choice and streusel topping.

Punch dough down and turn out onto a greased 14-inch pizza pan or 10 by 15-inch jelly roll pan; cover with inverted bowl and let rest for 5 to 10 minutes. Pat dough out to fit the pan, cover evenly with filling. Sprinkle an even layer of streusel atop filling. Let rise until puffy (about 20 minutes).

Bake in a 375° oven for 25 minutes or until crust and streusel are golden brown. Let cool for 20 minutes. Serve warm; or cool completely, cover, and keep at room temperature until the next day. To reheat, cover loosely with foil, bake in a 350° oven for 15 minutes. Dust with powdered sugar before serving, if desired. Makes 12 to 16 servings.

Poppy seed filling. In a blender, whirl 1 cup **poppy seeds** and ⅓ cup whole blanched **almonds** until powdery. Transfer mixture to a small pan and add ⅔ cup **sugar**, ¼ teaspoon **ground nutmeg**, ½ cup **milk**, ½ teaspoon **grated lemon peel**, 1 tablespoon **lemon juice**, and 2 tablespoons **butter** or margarine. Cook over low heat, stirring, until mixture boils and thickens (10 to 15 minutes); cool to room temperature.

Apple filling. In a 2-quart pan, combine 5 cups cored, peeled, and chopped **tart cooking apple**; 2 tablespoons **lemon juice**, and 1 tablespoon **water**. Bring to a boil over medium heat; cover and simmer, stirring occasionally, until apples are just tender when pierced (8 to 10 minutes). In a small bowl, mix together ¾ cup **sugar**, 2 tablespoons all-purpose **flour**, ½ teaspoon **ground cinnamon**, and ¼ teaspoon **ground nutmeg**; stir into apples and cook, stirring until thickened. Remove from heat and cool to room temperature.

Cheese filling. In a bowl, beat 1 large package (8 oz.) **cream cheese** until fluffy; beat in ½ cup **sugar**, 1 **egg**, and 1 teaspoon each **grated lemon peel** and **vanilla**. Stir in ½ cup **golden raisins**.

Streusel topping. In a bowl, mix 1¼ cups **all-purpose flour**, ½ cup **powdered sugar**, 1 teaspoon **baking powder**, and ½ teaspoon **ground cinnamon**. Using a pastry blender or 2 knives, cut ½ cup firm **butter** or margarine into mixture until it forms coarse, moist crumbs that begin to clump together. Mix in ½ teaspoon **vanilla**.

Old-fashioned Cake Doughnuts

Fresh, warm doughnuts are an irresistible morning treat. You can make the dough the night before, then roll, cut, and fry the doughnuts in the morning.

About 3½ cups all-purpose flour
3 teaspoons baking powder
1 teaspoon *each* salt and ground nutmeg
¼ teaspoon *each* ground cloves and mace
4 eggs
⅔ cup sugar
⅓ cup milk
⅓ cup butter or margarine, melted and cooled
1 teaspoon *each* vanilla and grated lemon peel
1½ to 2 quarts salad oil for frying
Powdered sugar frosting (directions follow)
Flaked coconut or chopped nuts (optional)

In a bowl, stir 3 cups of the flour together with baking powder, salt, nutmeg, cloves, and mace. In a large mixing bowl, beat eggs on high speed until very light and fluffy. Gradually add sugar, beating until mixture is very thick and lemon-colored. Reduce speed to low, then blend in milk, butter, vanilla, and lemon peel.

Gradually beat flour mixture into egg mixture to form a stiff dough (if dough seems soft, beat in about ¼ cup of the remaining flour). Cover and refrigerate until very cold (2 hours or overnight).

When ready to shape doughnuts, divide dough in half; cover and refrigerate one half. Turn other half out onto a floured board and dust lightly with some of the remaining ¼ cup of flour. Roll dough out to ½-inch thickness. Using a well-floured 3-inch doughnut cutter, cut out doughnuts and holes (dip cutter in flour each time) and place slightly apart on a lightly floured baking sheet. Reroll and cut the scraps. Repeat with remaining half of dough. Let doughnuts and holes stand, uncovered, at room temperature for 15 to 20 minutes.

To fry doughnuts, pour 2 inches oil into a deep 2 or 4-quart pan and heat to 375°–400° on a deep-frying thermometer. Gently add 2 or 3 doughnuts or holes at a time and fry, turning often, until golden brown (about 1½ to 2 minutes). Lift from oil with a slotted spoon; drain on paper towels.

Serve plain or cool completely and spread with powdered sugar frosting and sprinkle flaked coconut or chopped nuts over frosting, if desired. Makes about 2 dozen doughnuts and holes.

Powdered sugar frosting. Blend together 3 cups unsifted **powdered sugar,** 2 tablespoons soft **butter** or margarine, ¼ teaspoon **vanilla,** and 2 or 3 tablespoons warm **water.** Makes enough frosting for 1 to 1½ dozen doughnuts.

Cinnamon Doughnut Twists

Add a bit of sweetness to your meal with these delicious and tempting sugar-and-spice, raised doughnut twists.

2 packages active dry yeast
¼ cup warm water (about 110°)
1½ cups milk
½ cup sugar
1 teaspoon salt
½ teaspoon ground cinnamon
⅓ cup butter or margarine, cut in pieces
2 eggs
About 5¼ cups all-purpose flour
1½ to 2 quarts salad oil for frying
1 cup sugar
4 teaspoons ground cinnamon

In a large bowl, dissolve yeast in water; let stand until bubbly. Meanwhile, in a medium-size pan, combine milk, the ½ cup sugar, salt, the ½ teaspoon cinnamon, and butter. Heat over medium heat to about 110° (butter does not need to melt completely). Add milk mixture, eggs, and 2 cups of the flour to yeast mixture. Beat until well blended and smooth. With a heavy-duty mixer or spoon, mix in 3 more cups of the flour until smooth (dough will be soft and sticky). Cover and let rise in a warm place until almost doubled (about 1 hour).

Beat dough with a spoon to expel air. Turn dough out onto a well-floured board (dough will be very sticky). Roll dough around to coat all over with flour so it won't stick to board. With a floured rolling pin, roll dough into a rectangle ½ inch thick, 8 inches wide, and 18 inches long. With a floured knife, cut dough crosswise into 1-inch strips.

To form each twist, fold one strip in half crosswise and, grasping folded end in one hand and loose ends in other hand, twist in opposite directions. Press two loose ends together to seal. Leave uncovered on floured board to rise (if room is warm), or transfer to floured pans and let rise in a warm place, uncovered, until almost doubled (about 20 to 30 minutes).

To fry doughnuts, pour about 1½ to 2 inches of salad oil into a deep frying pan or 5-quart pan and heat to 350° on a deep-frying thermometer. Gently add doughnuts, a few at a time, and fry, turning often until golden brown (about 3 minutes total). Lift from oil with a slotted spoon; drain on paper towels.

Mix the 1 cup sugar and the 4 teaspoons cinnamon together in a bag. Add warm doughnuts, 1 or 2 at a time, and shake to coat. Makes about 18.

SNUG BREAKFAST FOR TWO on a rainy Saturday morning: crisp bacon and soft-cooked eggs (page 20) are teamed with Quick Fruit Tarts (page 72) that are remarkably quick to prepare.

Seafood, Poultry, Meat & other brunch surprises

Pizza for breakfast! Why not? You can serve anything for breakfast or brunch. And everyone loves a surprise —especially at breakfast time.

For a brunch surprise, try our pasta with a creamy cheese sauce, or skewered scallops and bacon with a rich béarnaise sauce, or even a quick and easy breakfast sandwich or pizza. The only thing that's essential for either breakfast or brunch is that the food be nutritional and good-looking.

This chapter invites you to be creative; it's full of delicious recipes and appealing menus, some dishes of which may surprise you if you've never thought of serving certain foods so early in the day. There are fresh-vegetable appetizers, on-the-run sandwiches, luscious seafood and poultry entrées, and delicious side dishes. We give you suggested menus plus some guidelines on creating menus of your own. You provide the colorful setting and the guest list. Have a glorious morning!

Dill Dip & Vegetable Appetizer

Crisp raw vegetables make perfect partners for the creamy dill dip. The vegetables as well as the dip can be prepared the night before.

- ⅔ cup *each* mayonnaise and sour cream
- 2 tablespoons chopped parsley
- 2½ teaspoons *each* dill weed and minced onion
- 1 teaspoon seasoned salt
  Cherry tomatoes
  Carrot and celery sticks
  Radish rounds
  Cauliflowerets

In a small bowl, blend mayonnaise and sour cream. Add parsley, dill weed, onion, and salt; blend well. Cover and refrigerate for at least 4 hours or until next day. Serve chilled, surrounded by tomatoes, carrots, celery, radishes, and cauliflowerets. Makes about 1⅓ cups.

Fish Spread Appetizer

The busy hostess or host will appreciate this versatile appetizer that's so quick to make.

- 1 can (about 7 oz.) chunk-style tuna, shrimp, or crab, drained; or ½ pound shrimp or crab meat
- 1 package (3 oz.) cream cheese, softened
- 1 clove garlic, minced or pressed
- 1 teaspoon lemon juice
  Assorted unsalted crackers
  Melba toast
  Crisp vegetables, (such as celery and carrot sticks, zucchini spears, cherry tomatoes, and cucumber rounds)

Flake tuna with a fork (finely chop shrimp or crab). In a small bowl, blend cream cheese, garlic, and lemon juice. Add fish and blend thoroughly. If you have a food processor, put all the ingredients in at one time and process until blended. Cover and chill for at least 1 hour or until next day.

To serve, mound the spread on a serving plate. Surround spread with crackers, Melba toast, and assorted vegetables.

Pasta with Sauce Supreme

Though this is one of the quickest sauces you can make for any of the Italian pasta shapes, it also is one of the most delicious.

The sauce is good with ordinary spaghetti or macaroni, but especially glorious with special shapes (often available frozen), such as tortellini, ravioli, or gnocchi. Tagliarini or wide egg noodles are also suitable. If you use fettuccine (medium wide noodles — also available frozen), the result is a deluxe version of Fettuccine Alfredo.

      4 tablespooons butter or margarine
    1½ cups whipping cream
      ½ teaspoon freshly grated (or ground) nutmeg
      4 cups hot, cooked, drained pasta such as fresh egg
            noodles, fettuccine, tagliarini, tortellini, ravioli,
            or gnocchi
      1 egg yolk
      ¾ cup freshly grated Parmesan cheese
         Freshly grated nutmeg and freshly grated Parmesan
            cheese

In a large pan over medium heat, melt butter with cream and the ½ teaspoon nutmeg. Stir in cooked pasta; quickly bring cream mixture to a boil; gently stir occasionally. Let boil rapidly for 1 to 2 minutes; remove pan from heat.

Beat egg yolk lightly and blend a little of the hot pasta mixture with egg yolk. Stir egg yolk-pasta mixture and the ¾ cup cheese back into hot pasta; blend well. Serve at once; offer additional nutmeg and cheese at table. Makes 4 main-dish servings.

Pasta with Carbonara Sauce

Beaten raw egg is the secret of this delicate and delicious sauce; it coats the spaghetti and causes the bits of cheese and meat to cling evenly. For a showy presentation, assemble it at the table.

      ¼ pound mild Italian sausages
      ¼ pound prosciutto or cooked ham, thinly sliced
      4 tablespoons butter or margarine
      3 eggs
      ½ cup *each* minced parsley and freshly grated
            Parmesan cheese
      8 ounces hot, cooked, drained spaghetti
         Grated Parmesan cheese
         Freshly ground black pepper

Remove casings from sausages and crumble meat into a wide frying pan. Finely chop prosciutto; combine half of it with sausage; set aside remaining half. Add 2 tablespoons of the butter to pan and cook, uncovered, over medium-low heat until sausage is lightly browned and edges of prosciutto are curled. Remove from heat and stir remaining half of prosciutto into cooked sausage mixture.

If made ahead, you can cover and refrigerate at this time. Reheat at serving time and transfer to a large serving bowl.

For a dramatic presentation, complete preparations at table. In a small bowl, beat eggs well. Have ready: hot meat mixture and, in separate containers,

the remaining 2 tablespoons butter, parsley, and the ½ cup cheese. Add hot spaghetti to meat mixture. Add butter and parsley; mix quickly to blend. Pour in eggs at once and quickly lift and mix spaghetti to coat well with egg. Sprinkle in the ½ cup cheese and a dash of pepper; mix thoroughly. Serve with additional cheese at the table. Makes 4 servings.

Carrot & Zucchini Medley

(Pictured on page 35)

You have here a savory blend of vegetables that makes a delicious filling for individual omelets (page 34), Dutch babies (page 44), or baked potato boats (page 79). You might also want to serve this dish alongside fluffy scrambled eggs (page 20).

      2 tablespoons butter or margarine
      1 large onion, thinly sliced
      1 pound *each* carrots and zucchini, cut in
            ¼-inch-thick slanting slices
      1 tablespoon chopped parsley
      ¾ teaspoon *each* salt and summer savory

In a wide frying pan over medium heat, melt butter. Add onion and cook, stirring occasionally, until limp and golden (about 15 minutes). Add carrots and cook for 3 minutes; stir in zucchini and cook for an additional 5 minutes, stirring occasionally until vegetables are just crisp-tender. Stir parsley, salt, and savory into vegetables. Makes 5 or 6 servings.

Marinated Mushroom Salad

(Pictured on page 27)

Fresh mushrooms and plump cherry tomatoes marinate in an oil and vinegar dressing for a light and refreshing brunch salad. With creamy scrambled eggs (page 26) in baked potato boats (page 79), this colorful salad makes wonderful brunch fare.

      1 cup salad oil
      2 teaspoons salt
    2½ teaspoons *each* dry basil and Dijon mustard
      ½ teaspoon *each* pepper and paprika
      5 tablespoons white wine vinegar
      4 teaspoons lemon juice
      2 pounds mushrooms, sliced
    1½ cups thinly sliced green onions, including some
            green tops
      1 basket cherry tomatoes, washed, and stems
            removed

In a large bowl, combine oil, salt, basil, mustard, pepper, paprika, vinegar, and lemon juice. Beat with a fork until well blended. Mix in mushrooms and

(Continued on page 79)

green onions; cover and marinate at room temperature, stirring occasionally, for about 1 hour or until serving time. Just before serving, mix in tomatoes. Makes 8 to 12 servings.

Easy Spinach-stuffed Mushrooms

Puffs of spinach soufflé crown large mushroom caps for a side dish that will dress up the simplest of foods, such as fluffy scrambled eggs or a plain omelet. For a buffet keep the mushrooms hot on a warming tray and serve with an array of breakfast cheeses, crusty rolls, and fresh fruit.

12   **mushrooms, 1½ to 2 inches in diameter**
4   **tablespoons butter or margarine, melted**
2   **tablespoons fine dry bread crumbs**
3   **tablespoons grated Parmesan cheese**
1   **package (12 oz.) frozen spinach soufflé, thawed**

Wash and carefully remove stems from mushrooms; reserve for other uses. Dip caps in melted butter and place them slightly apart, hollow side up, in a 9-inch-square baking pan.

Stir bread crumbs and 2 tablespoons of the cheese into soufflé; blend well. Fill mushroom hollows evenly with soufflé mixture. Sprinkle remaining 1 tablespoon of cheese evenly over mushrooms. Bake, uncovered, in a 400° oven for 20 minutes. Serve hot. Makes 6 servings of 2 each.

Tomato variation. Cut 3 small firm **tomatoes** in half crosswise. Leaving a ½-inch shell (be careful not to cut through bottom), scoop out pulp from each tomato half. (Save pulp and juice for other uses.) Invert tomato shells on paper towels to drain. Place tomato shells, hollow side up, in a greased 9-inch-square baking pan. Fill hollows with **soufflé mixture** and top with **cheese** as above. Bake as for mushrooms. Makes 6 servings.

Baked Potato Boats

(Pictured on page 27)

These edible containers make handy holders for creamy scrambled eggs (page 26), carrot & zucchini medley (page 77), or a variety of different fillings. You bake the potatoes, scoop out the pulp, then bake the potato shells until crisp and golden.

6   **medium-size russet potatoes**
½   **cup (¼ lb.) butter or margarine**
    Salt and pepper to taste

Scrub potatoes well and pat dry. Rub skins with 2 tablespoons of the butter, then prick each potato with a fork. Bake in a 425° oven for about 1 hour or until potatoes "give" when squeezed.

Cut each potato in half lengthwise, leaving a ¼-inch shell; scoop out pulp. (Save pulp for another use, such as mashed potatoes.) Put shells on a baking sheet. Melt remaining 6 tablespoons butter and brush inside of each potato shell with some of the butter. Sprinkle each with salt and pepper. At this point you can refrigerate shells until next day.

Return shells to oven and bake an additional 20 to 30 minutes or until shells are crisp and golden. Spoon in a hot filling (suggestions are in recipe introduction) and serve immediately. Makes 12 potato boats.

Quick Breakfast Quesadillas

Mexican cooks have many ways of stuffing a tortilla. What they call a quesadilla (keh-sah-thee-ya) resembles a grilled cheese sandwich. A good cheese that melts well is the basic filling; any other addition is at the discretion of the cook. Our version uses flour tortillas, but instead of frying, we bake them in a very hot oven to melt the cheese and crisp the tortillas. With a glass of citrus juice, these make great entrées to eat on the run when time is short.

1   **flour tortilla (about 8-inch size)**
½   **cup shredded Cheddar or jack cheese, or a mixture of both**
1   **tablespoon chopped, seeded, canned green chile (optional)**

Cover half the tortilla with cheese, to within ½ inch of edge. Add green chile, if used. Fold uncovered half of tortilla over cheese; place filled tortilla on a baking sheet. Place in a preheated 450° oven for 5 minutes or until cheese is melted and tortilla is lightly browned. Serve immediately. Makes 1 serving.

Quesadilla variations. You can substitute a different cheese, but pick one that melts easily, such as Swiss, American, or teleme.

For spicier quesadillas, drizzle 1 tablespoon **taco sauce** over cheese before folding.

For a meat filling, use only ¼ cup of the cheese and add 1 slice or about ¼ cup diced **cooked chicken**, turkey or beef.

SPICY GUACAMOLE (an avocado mixture) joins crisp vegetables and chopped eggs to fill these hearty pocket bread sandwiches called Avocado-wiches (page 80). Orange-Beef Broth (page 88) makes a nice winter accompaniment.

Breakfast Tortillas

Flour tortillas are dipped in an egg mixture and fried like French toast. At the table, each person spoons various condiments over a fried tortilla, then rolls it up to eat. To speed up preparation time for this early morning treat, the condiments, except for the avocado, can be placed in their individual bowls, covered, and refrigerated the night before.

12 to 16 strips bacon, crisply cooked, drained, and crumbled
2 cups (8 oz.) shredded sharp Cheddar cheese
8 green onions, thinly sliced
1 can (about 7 oz.) red chile salsa
2 firm, ripe avocados
1 tablespoon lemon juice
4 eggs
1 teaspoon salt
1 tablespoon milk
About 3 tablespoons butter or margarine
8 flour tortillas (about 8 inches in diameter)

Place bacon, cheese, onions, and salsa in individual serving bowls. Peel, pit, and dice avocados; coat with lemon juice and place in a serving bowl.

In a pie pan or a flat, rimmed dish (about 9 inches in diameter), beat together eggs, salt, and milk. In a wide frying pan over medium heat, melt 1 teaspoon of the butter. Dip a tortilla in egg mixture, drain briefly over dish, then fry in butter for about 1 minute on each side or until golden brown. Repeat until all tortillas are cooked, melting about 1 teaspoon butter in pan for each one. Stack tortillas between paper towels and keep warm until all are cooked.

Serve tortillas hot at table; pass condiments to spoon onto them. Roll up to eat. Makes 4 servings of 2 each.

Chile Ham Strata Sandwiches

When baked in the oven, savory French toast sandwiches puff up in ramekins almost like miniature soufflés. They are easy to assemble and can be prepared a day ahead. Serve with a fresh fruit salad and a hot beverage.

1 can (4 oz.) whole green chiles
1 cup (about 4 oz.) finely chopped cooked ham
2 cups (8 oz.) shredded jack or sharp Cheddar cheese
8 slices day-old firm white bread
6 eggs
2 cups milk
½ teaspoon *each* chili powder and dry mustard

Drain chiles, pat dry, and remove seeds, if desired. Finely chop chiles and mix with ham and 1 cup of the cheese. Divide mixture into 4 equal parts and spread over 4 of the bread slices. Top with remaining 4 bread slices to make 4 sandwiches. Place each sandwich in a well-buttered shallow ramekin (1½ to 2-cup size).

Lightly beat eggs, then beat in milk, chili powder, and dry mustard. Pour egg mixture evenly over sandwiches; cover and refrigerate for at least 2 hours or until next day.

To bake, uncover and sprinkle sandwiches with remaining 1 cup cheese. Set ramekins on a baking sheet and bake, uncovered, in a 350° oven for 40 to 45 minutes or until egg mixture is set and sandwiches are puffed in the center. Let stand for about 5 minutes before serving. Makes 4 servings.

Avocadowiches

(Pictured on page 78)

Resembling a Mexican taco, these pocket bread sandwiches are chock-full of fresh vegetables, hard-cooked eggs, and cheese—all bound together with a spicy avocado mixture. You can make the avocado mixture as spicy as you like for this brunch treat. The pocket bread (also called peda or pita bread) is available in most supermarkets or in Middle Eastern delicatessens.

In winter, accompany avocadowiches with hot orange-beef broth (page 88), in summer with spiced orange tea cooler (page 12). Serve squares of fresh apple coffee cake (page 71) for the finale.

1 large, firm, ripe avocado
1 tablespoon lemon juice
½ cup thinly sliced green onion
1 can (2¼ oz.) sliced ripe olives, drained
2 hard-cooked eggs, chopped
1 small tomato, peeled, seeded, and chopped
½ cup *each* shredded Cheddar cheese and diced celery
Garlic salt and liquid hot pepper seasoning
4 or 5 pocket breads, halved
3 cups shredded iceberg lettuce

Peel, pit, and slice avocado into a medium-size bowl. Add lemon juice; mash avocado with juice until well blended. Add onion, olives, eggs, tomato, cheese, and celery; stir to blend. Season to taste with garlic salt and hot pepper seasoning. If made ahead, cover and refrigerate for as long as 2 hours.

When ready to serve, stack bread halves (you should have 8 or 10 halves or pockets) on foil, wrap, and place in a 350° oven for 10 minutes or until heated through. Tuck a portion of the lettuce and then some of the avocado mixture into each warm bread half. Makes 8 to 10 pocket sandwiches.

Breakfast sandwiches: You get a packaged meal

Filled with meat and fruit, sandwiches can offer a fine solution to breakfast boredom. Because they make a neatly packaged meal that's quick to assemble and easy to eat, breakfast sandwiches appeal to hurried commuters. At the same time, they're a satisfying and nutritious start to the day.

Here are six sandwich suggestions to spark your creativity. You can vary the meats and fruits to suit your individual tastes and to take advantage of leftovers you have on hand—there's no limit to possible combinations.

Smoked Sausage & Apple Sandwich

Split 2 fully cooked **smoked sausage links** lengthwise. Place in a small pan over medium heat and brown lightly on all sides, adding a little **butter** or margarine if necessary. Lift out sausage; discard any drippings.

Add to pan about 1 tablespoon **butter** or margarine and about ½ small **apple,** peeled and thinly sliced. Sprinkle lightly with **sugar** and **ground cinnamon.** Cook until apple is golden brown on all sides.

Split, toast, and butter 1 **bagel.** Arrange sausages on one half; top with apple and remaining bagel half. Makes 1 sandwich.

Bacon & Banana Sandwich

In a small frying pan over medium heat, fry 2 or 3 strips **bacon** until crisp; drain well. Toast 2 slices **whole wheat bread** or firm white bread. Spread 1 slice with about 2 tablespoons **chunk-style peanut butter** and arrange bacon over top. Peel 1 small **banana** and slice lengthwise; arrange on bacon. Spread remaining toast with your favorite **fruit jelly** or with butter or margarine and place, jelly side down, on top of banana slices. Makes 1 sandwich.

jelly side down, on top of banana slices. Makes 1 sandwich.

Chicken & Orange Sandwich

Toast 2 slices **raisin bread** or firm white bread. Arrange sliced **cooked chicken** or turkey on 1 piece of toast and cover with fresh **orange slices,** canned mandarin oranges (drained), or fresh peach slices. Spread generously with **spiced apple yogurt** or vanilla-flavored yogurt, seasoned to taste with **ground ginger** or chopped crystallized ginger. Top with remaining toast. Makes 1 sandwich.

Ham & Pineapple Sandwich

Generously spread 2 slices **rye bread** with **butter** or margarine. Place 1 to 2 ounces sliced **cooked ham** on unbuttered side of 1 piece of bread. Top with a fresh or canned **pineapple slice** (well drained); sprinkle lightly with **ground nutmeg** and **brown sugar,** then top with 1 to 2 ounces sliced **jack cheese.** Cover with remaining bread slice, unbuttered side down. Cook in a sandwich grill until cheese is melted and bread is toasted. Makes 1 sandwich.

Braunschweiger & Prune Sandwich

Toast 2 slices **raisin bread** or whole wheat bread. Generously spread each slice with **apple butter;** cover 1 slice with 2 to 4 slices (*each* about ¼ inch thick) **braunschweiger** or liverwurst, and arrange halved moist-pack **pitted prunes** or dried apricots on top. Then add **butter lettuce** leaves and remaining toast, apple-butter-side down. Makes 1 sandwich.

Cottage Cheese & Strawberry Sandwich

Halve an **English muffin** and toast both halves. Place a slice of **cooked ham** on one half. Top ham with a generous spread of **cottage cheese;** top cheese with sliced **strawberries.** Then add **butter lettuce** leaves and remaining muffin half. Makes 1 sandwich.

Pizza Muffins

Savory individual pizzas make easy and quick eat-out-of-hand entrées. The thick meat sauce can be prepared the night before, and the English muffins can be halved and buttered ahead to make clean-up minimal. Quick avocado-grapefruit salad (page 5) makes a delicious accompaniment.

> 2 tablespoons butter or margarine
> 1 cup chopped onion
> 2 cloves garlic, minced or pressed
> 1½ pounds lean ground beef
> 1 cup catsup
> 2 tablespoons chili powder
> 1 can (2¼ oz.) sliced ripe olives, drained
> 6 English muffins, halved, buttered, and toasted
> About 1½ cups (6 oz.) shredded jack cheese

In a medium-size frying pan over medium heat, melt butter. Add onion and garlic; cook until onion is limp. Add beef and cook until browned and crumbly; drain off fat. Stir in catsup, chili powder, and olives. If made ahead, cover and refrigerate; reheat when needed.

Arrange muffin halves, cut side up, on a shallow baking pan.

Evenly divide hot meat mixture among the twelve muffin halves; top with cheese. Place in a preheated broiler about 6 inches from heat just until cheese melts. Makes 12 open-faced sandwiches.

Torta Rustica

(Pictured on opposite page)

By its very name, this savory Milanese tart suggests the ideal setting for its enjoyment: a country picnic. Equally good for a patio brunch, torta rustica is essentially a baked sandwich. Serve it hot, warm, cold, or reheated. Soups or salads are ideal companions.

> 1 package (13¾ oz.) hot yeast roll mix plus water and egg as specified on the box
> 1 filling (3 choices follow)
> 1 egg, lightly beaten

Prepare hot yeast roll mix as directed on the package. After the dough has risen, turn onto a lightly floured board and knead to expel air bubbles.

Divide dough in half; roll one portion on floured board into a 9-inch round. Fit dough in bottom of a greased 9 by 1½-inch layer cake pan with removable bottom. Cover evenly with filling.

Shape remaining portion of dough in one of the following ways:

Lattice: Roll dough into a 9-inch square and cut in strips about 1 inch wide. Weave strips over filling in a lattice pattern, tucking ends of dough down around filling at pan rim.

Wedges: Roll dough into a 9-inch round; cut into 8 wedges. Arrange wedges side by side on filling, with tips meeting in the center.

Circles: Roll dough into a 10-inch round. With a floured 2½-inch doughnut cutter cut 8 or 9 pieces; separate rings and center pieces. Gather scraps and reroll dough into a piece large enough to cut 3 or 4 more rounds, or a total of 10 to 12. Arrange all but one ring around edge of filling; place remaining ring in middle, then fit the little round center pieces around circle in middle.

Lightly cover shaped dough and set in a warm place for about 30 to 40 minutes or until puffy looking. Uncover and gently brush top with beaten egg.

Bake on lowest rack in a 350° oven for 35 to 40 minutes or until bread is richly browned (the spinach and ricotta version is very moist and requires maximum baking time.)

Cool bread in pan on wire rack for about 5 minutes, then remove pan rim. Serve warm or at room temperature; or cool, cover, and refrigerate to serve later. To reheat, wrap chilled bread in foil and bake in a 350° oven for 40 minutes (it takes as long to reheat as to bake). Cut in wedges. Makes 6 to 8 servings.

Spinach and ricotta filling. Wash and drain thoroughly enough **fresh spinach** leaves to make 1 cup, packed. Mince very finely with a knife or food processor. Blend spinach with 1 cup **ricotta cheese,** ½ cup grated **Parmesan cheese,** 1 **egg yolk,** ½ teaspoon **garlic salt,** and ⅛ teaspoon **pepper.**

Tuna and cheese filling. Thinly slice 1 small **onion,** separate into rings, and place in a frying pan with 1 tablespoon **olive oil.** Add ¼ cup finely chopped **green or red bell pepper** and cook, stirring, until onion is lightly browned. Remove from heat and add 1 can (about 7 oz.) chunk-style **tuna,** drained; ½ teaspoon **salt,** and ¼ teaspoon **oregano leaves;** stir to break apart tuna. Distribute filling on dough as directed; cover with 1 cup shredded **fontina** or jack cheese.

Sausage and tomato filling. Remove casings from ¾ pound **mild Italian sausages** and chop meat coarsely. In a wide frying pan over medium heat, cook meat until browned; remove from heat and spoon out and discard fat. Blend with meat ¼ cup finely chopped **parsley** and 2 tablespoons grated **Parmesan cheese.** Distribute filling on dough as directed, then top with ½ cup well-drained, canned, sliced **baby tomatoes,** and 1 cup (4 oz.) shredded **mozzarella cheese.**

TORTA RUSTICA is the Milanese name for this savory and hearty supersandwich filled with spinach and cheese. Serve it hot, warm, or cold accompanied by chilled tomato juice and fresh grapes. The recipe—with a choice of fillings—is on this page.

Tuna Marinara Muffins

A delicious topping of tuna, artichoke hearts, and tangy tomato sauce crowns these open-faced sandwiches. The topping can be cooked the night before and reheated while you prepare the English muffins. For a buffet, keep these hot on a warming tray.

    1 can (about 7 oz.) chunk-style tuna
    1 clove garlic, minced or pressed
    1 can (8 oz.) tomato sauce
    1 teaspoon sugar
    ½ teaspoon oregano leaves
    1 jar (6 oz.) marinated artichoke hearts, drained
    1 tablespoon finely chopped parsley
    3 English muffins, halved
    6 slices (about 6 oz.) Swiss or mozzarella cheese
    3 tablespoons grated Parmesan cheese

Drain 1 tablespoon oil from tuna into a saucepan; discard remaining oil and set tuna aside. Over medium heat, cook garlic in oil until limp. Add tomato sauce, sugar, and oregano; simmer for about 15 minutes.

Cut artichoke hearts in half and stir into sauce. Gently stir in parsley and tuna; keep warm while preparing muffins. If made ahead, cover and refrigerate at this point and reheat when needed.

Arrange muffin halves, cut side up, in a shallow baking pan. Place in broiler about 6 inches from heat until lightly toasted. Place a slice of Swiss cheese over each muffin half; broil 6 inches from heat just until cheese melts. Spoon the hot tuna mixture evenly over each half; sprinkle each with some of the Parmesan cheese. Makes 6 open-faced sandwiches.

Sausage Bread Ring

Frozen bread dough is rolled into a rectangle and then wrapped around a spicy sausage filling for a quick and hearty brunch. You can make the bread several weeks ahead and freeze it, or prepare it early on the day of your brunch.

    1 loaf (1 lb.) frozen bread dough
    1 pound mild Italian sausage
    2 eggs
    ½ teaspoon Italian herb dressing (or ¼ teaspoon *each* dry basil and oregano leaves)
    1½ cups (6 oz.) shredded mozzarella or jack cheese
    1 tablespoon grated Parmesan cheese

Let bread defrost in refrigerator overnight, or let stand at room temperature for 2 to 2½ hours.

Remove sausage from casing and cook in a frying pan set over medium-high heat until brown and crumbly. Remove pan from heat, drain off fat, and let sausage cool completely. Beat 1 egg; add to sausage along with herb seasoning and mozzarella and stir to blend.

On a lightly floured board, roll and stretch bread dough into a 6 by 18-inch rectangle. Spoon sausage mixture evenly over dough to within ½-inch of edges. Then roll up dough, starting from one of the long sides, and pinch seam firmly to seal.

On a large greased baking sheet, shape roll into a ring. Pinch ends together firmly to seal. Slash top of ring with a sharp knife, making ½-inch-deep cuts about 1½ inches apart. Beat remaining egg and brush over bread ring; sprinkle with Parmesan cheese. Cover and let rise in a warm place until doubled (about 35 minutes).

Bake bread in a 350° oven for 30 minutes or until golden brown. Serve warm; or cool to room temperature, wrap securely in foil, and freeze. To reheat, unwrap and defrost the bread completely, then place on a baking sheet. Cover bread loosely with foil and heat in a 350° oven for 15 minutes. Uncover and continue heating for 15 minutes more or until bread is hot throughout. Makes 8 to 10 servings.

Bacon & Cheese Breakfast Pizza

Pizza for breakfast may sound strange, but this isn't an ordinary pizza. It's more like a thin quiche combining breakfast favorites of bacon and cheese in a custard-filled pastry crust. Accompany with apricot citrus juice (page 10) — it can be prepared the night before.

    Pastry for a single-crust 9-inch pie
    ½ pound sliced bacon, crisply cooked, drained, and crumbled
    2 cups (8 oz.) shredded Swiss cheese
    4 eggs
    1⅓ cups sour cream
    2 tablespoons chopped parsley

Preheat oven to 425°. On a lightly floured board, roll out pastry to fit a 12-inch pizza pan. Fit pastry into pan, pressing edges against pan sides and trimming even with top. Bake crust on lowest rack in preheated oven for 5 minutes. Gently press down any bubbles in crust; cool before filling.

Sprinkle bacon and cheese over crust. In a medium-size bowl, lightly beat eggs; stir in sour cream and parsley until smooth; pour over pizza.

(Continued on page 87)

Granola parfaits: A delicious morning treat

(Pictured on page 86)

Children and adults alike delight in these nutritious and appetizing granola parfaits. The layered assembly of granola, yogurt, and fruit is quick, and cleanup is easy.

The granola cereal, which forms the bottom layer of these luscious parfaits, you can make yourself.

The second layer of our parfait features tangy, unflavored yogurt. But you can also top granola with cottage cheese, sour cream, or our version of fruited yogurt (recipe below). For flavor balance, the yogurt should be slightly tart because the granola is slightly sweet.

To assemble parfaits: Spoon about ⅓ cup of granola into each glass; top with a few spoonfuls of unflavored or fruited yogurt, cottage cheese, or sour cream. Then spoon on fresh fruit. Repeat layers, if desired, and you have an irresistible treat. What a way to start the day!

Nutty Oat Granola

This simple, good-tasting mixture will have everyone raiding the granola canister.

    8 cups regular rolled oats
 1½ cups firmly packed brown sugar
 1½ cups regular wheat germ
    1 large package (8 oz.) shredded coconut
 1½ cups salted, hulled sunflower seeds or salted
        cashews
  ½ cup salad oil
  ¾ cup honey
    2 teaspoons vanilla

Stir to blend oats, sugar, wheat germ, coconut, and sunflower seeds. In a small pan, heat oil, honey, and vanilla, stirring, until bubbling. Thoroughly mix the liquids with the dry ingredients.

Grease 2 large 10 by 15-inch rimmed baking sheets, then divide cereal mixture between pans, spreading it out evenly.

Bake, uncovered, in a 325° oven for 15 to 20

minutes or until coconut is lightly browned, stirring two or three times with a wide spatula. Remove pans from oven; stir granola several times as it cools to prevent sticking. When thoroughly cool, store airtight. Makes 16 cups.

Six-grain Granola

Peanut butter gives added nutrition and flavor to this granola.

    3 cups regular rolled oats
    1 cup whole wheat flour
  ½ cup *each* cornmeal, rye flour, millet meal, and
        wheat germ
  ½ cup firmly packed brown sugar
  ⅓ cup *each* shredded coconut, hulled salted sun-
        flower seeds, and sesame seeds
 1½ teaspoons salt
  ½ cup creamy or chunk-style peanut butter
  ½ cup *each* salad oil and water
  ½ teaspoon vanilla

In a large mixing bowl, combine rolled oats, whole wheat flour, cornmeal, rye flour, millet, wheat germ, sugar, coconut, sunflower seeds, sesame seeds, and salt.

In a blender, combine peanut butter, oil, water, and vanilla; whirl until well combined. Add to the rolled oat mixture and mix well with your hands. Then crumble the mixture into a large broiler pan, forming an even layer. Bake, uncovered, in a 250° oven for 1 hour; stir every 20 minutes. Turn off oven; leave mixture in closed oven until completely cooled. Store airtight. Makes 9 cups.

Fruited Yogurt

Our recipe is not as sweet as purchased fruit yogurt. If you prefer a sweeter yogurt, add honey, a tablespoon at a time.

    1 quart (32 oz.) unflavored yogurt
    1 package (10 oz.) frozen presweetened berries or
        mixed fruit, thawed; or 1½ cups fresh sliced
        berries to which you add 2 tablespoons sugar
        and let stand for 1 hour to draw out juices
        Honey (optional)

In a large bowl, stir together yogurt and thawed fruit and juice. Sweeten with honey, 1 tablespoon at a time, if desired. Cover and refrigerate for at least 4 hours or overnight to blend flavors. Stir before serving. Makes about 5 cups.

To bake, return pizza to lowest oven rack and bake in a preheated 425° oven 20 to 25 minutes or until puffy and lightly browned. Let stand for 5 minutes before cutting. Makes 4 or 5 servings.

Sausage-Spinach Pizza Pie

A rich egg pastry is the base for this savory meat and vegetable pizza. In advance, you can line the baking pan with buttery crust, cover the crust with the sausage and cheese topping, and then refrigerate it until you're ready to bake. Serve hot or at room temperature with fruit.

1½ cups all-purpose flour
⅛ teaspoon salt
½ cup (¼ lb.) firm butter or margarine
1 egg
1 pound mild Italian sausages
1 pound mushrooms, thinly sliced
1 medium-size onion, finely chopped
1 package (about 10 oz.) frozen chopped spinach, thawed, and all moisture squeezed out
1 teaspoon lemon juice
½ teaspoon salt
⅛ teaspoon ground nutmeg
2 cups (8 oz.) shredded jack cheese
2 medium-size tomatoes

In a bowl, combine flour and the ⅛ teaspoon salt. With a pastry blender or with two knives, cut in butter until coarse crumbs form. Lightly beat egg and stir into flour mixture until mixture clings together. With your hands, form dough into a compact ball. Place dough on a lightly floured board; roll dough out to fit a 14-inch pizza pan or a 10 by 15-inch jelly roll pan. Fit pastry into pan, pressing edges against pan sides and trimming even with top; set aside.

Remove casings from sausages, crumble meat into a wide frying pan, and cook, uncovered, over medium-high heat until browned. Add mushrooms and onion; cook, stirring, until liquid evaporates. Remove from heat and add spinach, lemon juice, the ½ teaspoon salt, and nutmeg; stir until well blended.

Spread pastry evenly with sausage mixture. Sprinkle 1½ cups of the cheese evenly over sausage; reserve the remaining ½ cup cheese. If made ahead, you can cover and refrigerate at this point.

To bake, place pizza in a 450° oven for 15 minutes. While pizza is baking, slice tomatoes. Remove pizza

LUSCIOUS LAYERS of Nutty Oat Granola (page 85), unflavored yogurt, and fresh sliced berries make these granola parfaits a glorious morning treat.

from oven; top with tomato slices and sprinkle the reserved ½ cup cheese atop tomatoes. Return to oven for 5 more minutes or until cheese has melted and crust is lightly browned. Let stand for 5 minutes before cutting. Serve hot or at room temperature. Makes 6 to 8 servings.

Savory Cheese Pie

Light and nourishing, this double-crust, cheese and tomato pie makes a delightful winter brunch entrée. For easier cutting, cool the pie for 10 minutes before serving.

½ teaspoon black pepper
¼ teaspoon *each* dry mustard and paprika
Pastry mix for a double-crust 9-inch pie
2½ cups (10 oz.) shredded sharp Cheddar cheese
2 eggs
⅔ cup milk
¼ teaspoon salt
1½ tablespoons finely chopped onion
2 medium-size tomatoes, peeled and sliced
1 egg, lightly beaten

In a small bowl, stir together pepper, mustard, paprika, and pastry mix; prepare according to package directions. Divide pastry into 2 equal portions. Roll one portion out on a lightly floured board. Fit pastry over bottom and sides of a 9-inch pie pan. Distribute shredded cheese over pastry. Beat the 2 eggs with milk, salt, and onion; pour over cheese. Cover cheese with a layer of tomato slices. Roll remaining pastry out on a lightly floured board and cover filling. Seal, slash top, and crimp rim decoratively. Reserve scraps, reroll, cut out 2 or 3 leaf shapes and place on center of pie. Brush top with beaten egg. Bake in a 425° oven for 10 minutes; reduce heat to 325° and cook for 30 minutes longer or until well browned. Cool for 10 minutes before cutting. Makes 6 servings.

Easy Chicken Divan

This simplified version of classic chicken divan can be prepared in advance; the secret is in the sauce. The ingredients can easily be doubled and baked in a 9 by 13-inch baking dish for a buffet. Complement it with crusty rolls and fresh fruit.

1 package (10 or 12 oz.) frozen broccoli spears or chopped broccoli
3 cups shredded cooked chicken or turkey
1 can (10¾ oz.) condensed cream of chicken soup
¼ cup mayonnaise
1 cup (4 oz.) shredded Cheddar cheese

(Continued on page 89)

Soup for starters

Soup for breakfast or brunch, warm or cold—it's a nourishing way to start off a morning meal.

Lingonberry-Blueberry Soup

In the Scandinavian tradition, breakfast begins with a well-chilled fruit soup that you can make several days ahead. Look for canned lingonberries in the gourmet food section of your market.

    2   cups water
    3   tablespoons quick-cooking tapioca
    ½   cup sugar
    ¼   teaspoon salt
    2   sticks cinnamon, each about 1½ inches long
    1   teaspoon grated lemon peel
    ⅓   cup lemon juice
    1½ cups (about 8 oz.) frozen unsweetened blueberries
    1   jar (14 oz.) lingonberries
        Sour cream

In a saucepan, combine water, tapioca, sugar, salt, cinnamon, lemon peel, lemon juice, and blueberries. Over medium-high heat, bring mixture to a boil, stirring constantly; reduce heat and simmer, stirring occasionally, for 5 minutes. Remove from heat and stir in lingonberries and their liquid until blended. Cover and refrigerate until well chilled. Remove cinnamon sticks. Serve cold and pass a bowl of sour cream to spoon over individual servings. Makes 6 servings.

Orange-Beef Broth

(Pictured on page 78)

This intriguing hot soup has a subtle flavor and aroma. Serve it on a cold winter day with avocadowiches (page 80).

    2   large navel oranges
    3   tablespoons butter or margarine
    2   cans (10½ oz. *each*) condensed beef broth
    1   soup can water
    ½   cup orange juice
    1   teaspoon sugar
    2   whole cloves

Using a vegetable peeler, cut thin strips of zest (outer part of peel) from oranges. You need 6 strips, each about 1 inch long. Set aside to garnish soup servings.

With a sharp knife, cut away and discard all remaining peel, including white membrane, from oranges. Section fruit (work over pan to catch juices) and place in pan. Add butter and simmer for about 3 minutes.

Add beef broth, water, the ½ cup orange juice, sugar, and cloves. Bring to a boil; reduce heat and simmer, uncovered, for about 10 minutes; then press through a wire strainer.

Reheat when ready to serve. Add a twist of the reserved orange peel to each serving bowl or cup. Pour in the piping hot soup. Makes 6 small servings.

Icy Gazpacho

(Pictured on page 38)

There are many versions of this Spanish specialty. This one is best described as a cooling salad in soup form. It makes a refreshing opener for a hot-weather picnic brunch. You may want to serve it topped with croutons.

    1   cucumber
    ½   green pepper, seeded
    1   small onion
    2   tomatoes
    ½   avocado
    4   cups tomato juice
    3   tablespoons olive oil or salad oil
    2   tablespoons white wine vinegar
    ½   teaspoon oregano leaves
        Salt
        Ice cubes
        Seasoned croutons (optional)

Peel cucumber and cut in half, lengthwise. If seeds are large, scoop out with a spoon and discard. Coarsely chop cucumber. Finely chop green pepper and onion; add cucumber.

Peel tomatoes and cut into ¼-inch cubes. Peel avocado and cut into ½-inch cubes. In a bowl, combine tomato and avocado cubes, along with cucumber mixture. Add tomato juice, olive oil, vinegar, oregano, and salt to taste. Chill for at least 2 hours or until next day. To serve, ladle into bowls or cups and add 2 ice cubes to each bowl. Pass croutons to spoon atop each serving. Makes about 8 servings.

Cook broccoli according to package directions; drain thoroughly. Spread broccoli evenly over bottom of a buttered 9-inch-square baking dish. Evenly distribute chicken over broccoli. In a small bowl, blend together soup and mayonnaise; spread over chicken. Sprinkle cheese evenly over soup mixture. If made ahead, you can cover and refrigerate at this point, if you wish.

Bake, uncovered, in a 350° oven for about 30 minutes or until heated through and cheese is bubbly and brown. Makes 4 servings.

Gravlax with Sweet Mustard Sauce

Very popular throughout Scandinavia, this treatment of salmon resembles lightly smoked salmon or kosher-style lox. The procedure takes 24 hours; no cooking is involved — the salmon cures in a brine. You can serve thin slices of gravlax alone or on bagels with cream cheese. Our recipe includes directions for a sweet mustard sauce that is an excellent topping for gravlax served on slices of bread. You might also want to try gravlax as a main dish for a picnic, with potato or macaroni salad and sliced tomatoes. Fresh apple coffee cake (page 71) makes a delicious finale.

    1   teaspoon *each* dill weed and dill seed, or 1
        tablespoon finely chopped fresh dill
    2   tablespoons salt
    ¼   cup sugar
    12 whole black peppers
    1   or 2 center-section salmon fillets (about 2 lbs. total),
        without skin
        Sweet mustard sauce (directions follow)

In a small bowl, mix together dill weed and seed, salt, sugar, and black peppers. Rub mixture onto fish. Place salmon in a rimmed, flat-bottom dish that fits the salmon compactly. Cover and chill for 24 hours. During this time, spoon juices over fish occasionally. The salmon keeps for as long as a week in brine, but it gradually grows too salty to be enjoyable.

To serve, discard brine and slice fish thinly across the grain on the diagonal. Wrap in plastic wrap and refrigerate. It will keep for as long as 1 week. Makes 4 to 6 main dish servings or 8 to 12 sandwich fillings.

Sweet mustard sauce. In a small bowl, stir together 2 tablespoons **Dijon mustard**, 1 tablespoon **sugar**, 1½ tablespoons **white wine vinegar**, ½ teaspoon **salt**, and 1 teaspoon finely chopped fresh **dill** (or ¼ teaspoon dill weed). With a fork, gradually and smoothly beat in ⅓ cup **salad oil**. Makes about ⅔ cup.

Crab-stuffed Chicken Breasts

Boned chicken breasts are flattened, topped with a crab filling, rolled, and baked in this make-ahead entrée. Delicious when accompanied by gingered tropical fruit plate (page 8) and cottage cheese pan rolls (page 71).

    4   whole chicken breasts (about 12 oz. *each*) halved,
        skinned, and boned
    4   tablespoons butter or margarine
    ½   cup thinly sliced green onion
    ¼   pound mushrooms, thinly sliced
    3   tablespoons all-purpose flour
    ¼   teaspoon thyme leaves
    ½   cup *each* chicken broth, milk, and dry white wine
        (or an additional ½ cup broth)
        Salt and pepper
    8   ounces crab meat or 1 can (about 7 oz.) crab, drained
    ⅓   cup *each* finely chopped parsley and fine dry bread
        crumbs
    1½ cups (6 oz.) shredded Swiss cheese

Pound chicken breasts between wax paper until ¼ inch thick; set aside.

In a medium-size frying pan over medium heat, melt butter. Add onions and mushrooms and cook until onion is limp. Stir in flour and thyme; cook until bubbly. Gradually stir in broth, milk, and wine; cook, stirring, until sauce thickens. Remove from heat and season to taste with salt and pepper.

In a small bowl, stir ¼ cup of the sauce together with crab, parsley, and bread crumbs. Spread equal amounts of filling over each chicken piece. Roll chicken around crab filling to enclose. Place rolls, seam side down, in a greased 9 by 13-inch baking dish.

Pour remaining sauce over rolls; sprinkle with cheese. If made ahead, cover and refrigerate until next day. To bake, place, covered, in a 400° oven for 30 minutes (40 minutes, if refrigerated) or until chicken is no longer pink when slashed. Makes 4 to 8 servings.

Creamy Ham with Artichokes & Mushrooms

(Pictured on page 67)

For a special Easter or garden brunch, try this rich, flavorful filling in hollowed-out brioches, purchased patty shells, or popovers. And what is so helpful — you can prepare the filling up to a day ahead. Serve with a simple garnish of carrot curls and radish roses.

(Continued on next page)

6 tablespoons butter or margarine
½ pound mushrooms, sliced
¼ teaspoon *each* dry mustard and thyme leaves
3 tablespoons all-purpose flour
1½ cups milk
2½ cups (10 oz.) shredded Cheddar cheese
⅛ teaspoon pepper
1 tablespoon dry sherry
1 can (8½ oz.) quartered artichoke hearts, drained
2 to 3 cups cubed cooked ham
Salt to taste
6 to 8 brioches (page 66) or purchased patty shells, hollowed out; or popovers (page 64)

In a wide frying pan over medium heat, melt 2 tablespoons of the butter. Add mushrooms and cook until liquid evaporates. Add remaining 4 tablespoons butter, as well as mustard and thyme. When butter melts, stir in flour and cook until bubbly. Gradually stir in milk and cook, stirring constantly, until sauce boils and thickens. Add cheese, pepper, and sherry; stir until cheese melts, then remove from heat. Stir in artichoke hearts and ham. Season to taste with salt. If made ahead, you can cool, cover, and refrigerate at this point.

To serve, reheat, stirring gently over medium-low heat. Meanwhile, with a spoon, gently hollow out each brioche or patty shell, leaving a ¼-inch-thick shell. (Be careful not to cut through sides or bottom.) Spoon filling into shells or transfer filling to a chafing dish and let guests help themselves. Makes 6 to 8 servings.

Scallops & Bacon Skewers

(Pictured on opposite page)

Scallops, delicate yet distinctively flavored shellfish, are skewered with bacon strips and broiled to perfection. Top them with luscious bearnaise sauce for an easy entrée. A few simple accompaniments — a dry white wine, chilled melon wedges, and crusty rolls — turn this delightful entrée into a satisfying feast. Buttermilk coffee cake (page 71) makes a fitting dessert.

12 strips bacon
2 pounds scallops
6 tablespoons butter or margarine, melted with 1 teaspoon *each* chervil and paprika
Bearnaise sauce (recipe at right)

Place separated bacon strips on a cold rack in a rimmed pan. Partially broil bacon about 6 inches from heat. Remove from heat; drain slightly on paper towels.

Wash scallops and pat dry with paper towels. On each of 8 skewers, alternately thread bacon and scal-

lops; bacon will form S-curves around scallops. Brush with flavored butter. Broil 6 inches from heat for 5 to 7 minutes per side, brushing with butter often, until bacon is crisp and scallops are cooked through. While scallops are cooking, make bearnaise sauce. Place in a bowl and pass at the table to spoon atop skewers. Makes 4 to 8 servings.

Steaks with Bearnaise Sauce

On a leisurely morning, brunch can be quite an elaborate affair when you treat guests to breakfast-size steaks with bearnaise sauce, fresh orange juice, crusty potato casserole (page 24), and chilled melon wedges.

2 tablespoons butter or margarine
1 teaspoon *each* chopped parsley and minced onion
4 small (3 or 4 oz. *each*) tender boneless beef steaks (fillets, rib or market steaks, or cube steaks)
Quick blender bearnaise sauce (directions follow)

In a small pan over medium heat, melt butter. Add parsley and onion; cook until onion is limp. Remove from heat. Brush onion butter over one side of each steak. Grill or broil steaks to desired degree of doneness, turning once and brushing with the remaining butter. While steaks are cooking, make bearnaise sauce. Place steaks on individual plates and top with 2 tablespoons of sauce; pass remaining sauce at the table. Makes 4 servings.

Quick blender bearnaise sauce. In a small pan over medium heat, simmer 1 tablespoon **minced chives** or green onions and ½ teaspoon **tarragon leaves** in 2 tablespoons **white wine vinegar**, stirring, until liquid evaporates. In a blender or food processor, place 1 **egg**, 1 teaspoon **Dijon mustard**, 1 tablespoon **lemon juice**, and the chive mixture; whirl at high speed until well blended. With blender running, add 1 cup melted **butter** or margarine, a few drops at a time at first, then increase flow to a slow, steady stream. Serve at once. Makes 1 to 1½ cups.

SEAFOOD DELICACIES for an outdoor brunch are these barbecued Scallops & Bacon Skewers. Spoon luscious Bearnaise Sauce on top and accompany with chilled melon wedges. The recipes are on this page.

Menu ideas: How to put it all together

"What an attractive table!"..."That was delicious."... "How do you produce meals that are nutritious and so good at the same time?"

Breakfasts and brunches win comments like these when you've planned them carefully, and careful planning begins with a well-thought-out menu. The end product is delectable food and a pleasing, relaxed atmosphere—essential to a successful breakfast or brunch.

You can develop your menu around a theme— a Mexican fiesta brunch, for example, or a Christmas buffet. Or try an on-location meal, like a back-yard breakfast for the kids, or brunch at the seashore or in your own garden. You can also plan a menu around one main dish, then choose complementary food to go with it.

Take into consideration the color, flavor, shape, temperature, and texture of each food you include on the menu. For example, serve chewy, crisp, and soft foods together; have some foods hot, others cool or cold. One spicy food is usually enough, and it's wise to avoid too many sweet dishes on the same menu.

Create a special mood with decorations and plates appropriate to the theme or food you've chosen. For buffet-style entertaining, plan food that can be served attractively at room temperature or can be kept hot on warming trays or in chafing dishes.

We give you suggested menus below, to be followed in their entirety, if you wish. But don't be limited by them—you'll also want to select the recipe combinations or single recipes that appeal to you or suit your needs. Most important: Let your imagination go...be innovative and have fun.

No-cook Deli Brunch

(Pictured on page 94)

A glorious outdoor brunch can be a breeze when you take advantage of the large selection of ready-to-eat delicacies from a grocery store or delicatessen. You can present an abundance of good food and still have no pots or pans to wash. Select a few appetizers, your entrée, and dessert, then find a sunny location and enjoy a leisurely feast.

Antipasto   Caviar   Herring
Pâté with Assorted Crackers
Assorted Cold Meats & Cheeses
Marinated Artichokes   Pickled Vegetables
Ripe Olives   Sweet Pickles
Assorted Breads
Cookies & Chocolates
Wine   Orange Juice   Apple Juice

Elegant Garden Brunch

Springtime brings fair weather and makes your garden a wonderful entertaining center for a leisurely brunch. This menu lets you relax and enjoy your guests, because everything can be prepared the night before.

Fresh Fruit Plate
Easy Chicken Divan (page 87)
Carrot Curls   Radish Roses
Croissants (page 68)   **Butter Balls**
Buttermilk Coffee Cake (page 71)
Coffee or Tea

Breakfast-on-the-Run

When time is short, consider this simple breakfast—it satisfies early morning hunger pangs but takes only minutes to prepare. While you're getting dressed, you can be preheating the oven for the quesadillas.

Chilled Tomato Juice
Quick Breakfast Quesadillas (page 79)
Fresh Fruit

Special Guest Breakfast

When friends or relatives spend the weekend, the thought of getting up early to prepare a company breakfast can sometimes seem overwhelming. The simple make-ahead menu featured below, gives you an easy way to serve eggs and sausage with a special touch. The breakfast finale—fruit-filled pineapple boats—can double as colorful centerpieces.

Scotch Eggs (page 26)   **Toasted English Muffins**
Pineapple Fruit Refresher (page 8)
Coffee, Tea, or Milk

An Italian Brunch

This hearty Mediterranean menu includes an omelet-like frittata with Italian sausages, accompanied by a moderately sweet, cakelike bread known in Italy as *panettone*. If you can't buy this Italian sweet bread, substitute toasted raisin bread. To warm the panettone, wrap it in foil and heat in a 325° oven for about 25 minutes, then cut it in wedges to serve. Fresh fruit, cheese, and *caffè latte* make a choice ending. Use Swiss cheese if fontina isn't available. To make the caffè latte, you simply pour equal portions of hot coffee and hot milk into cups or mugs; for continental flair, pour them simultaneously, a pitcher in each hand.

Basil Frittata with Italian Sausages
in Pepper Sauce (page 34)
Hot Panettone   Butter
Sliced Oranges   Grape Clusters
Fontina Cheese
Caffè Latte

Children's Picnic Breakfast

Youngsters will be delighted with this eat-out-of-hand picnic breakfast, and parents will relish the fact that it's easy and nutritious. Set the stage under a favorite back-yard tree and use paper plates to reduce cleanup time. Here's how to prevent banana chunks from browning: Cut them just before serving and sprinkle with lemon juice.

Pigs-in-a-Blanket (page 42)
Orange Wedges   Banana Chunks
Sweet Mini-muffins (page 63)
Milk

Mexican Fiesta Brunch

All the components for this colorful, healthful, and easy menu for four can be prepared a day ahead. Add ground cinnamon to the hot chocolate for a Mexican accent. For an even more authentic touch, serve this festive menu in colorful Mexican pottery and use bright decorations, including a piñata, to add to the special mood.

Avocados Huevos Rancheros (page 16)
Refried Beans   Warm Tortillas
Papaya & Pineapple Compote (page 5)
Hot Chocolate (page 15)

Brunch at the Seashore

(Pictured on page 38)

You can prepare this delicious totable meal a day ahead. The chilled gazpacho soup is a perfect prelude to torta rustica or individual cheese quiches. Accompaniments are simple: crisp vegetables, wine, fresh fruit of the season, and treats from the bakery for a sweet finale.

Gazpacho (page 88)
Torta Rustica (page 82)
or
Individual Cheese Quiches (page 39)
Crisp Raw Vegetables
Fresh Fruit   Sweet Treats
Wine

Christmas Buffet Brunch

Welcome Christmas brunch guests with a spiced fruit punch and our fish spread appetizer served with assorted crackers and crisp vegetables. Except for the creamy scrambled eggs and sausage patties, everything for this festive menu for twelve can be prepared a day in advance. The eggs and sausages can be prepared half an hour before you plan to serve them, and kept hot on warming trays. Swedish cardamom wreath makes a sweet and gala ending.

Hot Crimson Apple Punch (page 15)
Fish Spread Appetizer (page 76)
Assorted Crackers   Crisp Vegetables
Creamy Scrambled Eggs (page 26)   **Sausage Patties**
Marinated Mushroom Salad (page 77)
Crusty Rolls   Butter
Swedish Cardamom Wreath (page 72)
Coffee, Tea, or Milk

Hearty Winter Breakfast

You can prepare the apricot citrus and start the pancake batter for this substantial breakfast the night before. In the morning, while the pancakes are baking, cook the bacon.

Apricot Citrus (page 10)
Old-fashioned Oatmeal Pancakes (page 41)
Butter   Maple Syrup (page 52)
Crisp Bacon Strips
Coffee, Tea, or Milk

Index

*USY EPICURE'S DELIGHT is
array for a no-cook deli brunch.
ong the delicacies are Swiss cheese,
d salami, pickled red peppers and
iflower, marinated artichokes,
ring, olives, pickles, assorted
ds, cookies, wine, and fruit juice.
more suggestions, see the menu
age 92.*

A Handy Metric Conversion Table

To change	To	Multiply by
ounces (oz.)	grams (g)	28
pounds (lbs.)	kilograms (kg)	0.45
teaspoons	milliliters (ml)	5
tablespoons	milliliters (ml)	15
fluid ounces (fl. oz.)	milliliters (ml)	30
cups	liters (l)	0.24
pints (pt.)	liters (l)	0.47
quarts (qt.)	liters (l)	0.95
gallons (gal.)	liters (l)	3.8
inches	centimeters (cm)	2.5
Fahrenheit temperature (°F)	*Celsius temperature (°C)*	*5/9 after subtracting 32*